# Improve Your Reading

## Ron Fry

**KOGAN PAGE**

**Other books in this Kogan Page series:**
*Getting Organised*
*How to Study*
*Improve Your Memory*
*Improve Your Writing*
*Last Minute Study Tips*

**Forthcoming**
*Manage Your Time*
*Pass Any Test*
*Take Notes*
*Use Your Computer*

First published in 1996 in the USA by The Career Press,
3 Tice Road, PO Box 687, Franklin Lakes, NJ 07417
This European edition published 1997 by Kogan Page Ltd

Kogan Page Limited
120 Pentonville Road
London N1 9JN

**British Library Cataloguing in Publication Data**

A CIP record for this book is available from the British Library.

ISBN 0 7494 2348 X

Typeset by Jo Brereton, Primary Focus, Haslington, Cheshire
Printed and bound in Great Britain by Clays Ltd St Ives plc

# *Contents*

# INTRODUCTION
# Read on!

## So who are you?

A number of you are students, not just secondary school students but also college and university students.

Many of you reading this are adults. Some of you are returning to education; some of you left school a long time ago but have worked out that if you could learn now the study skills your teachers never taught you, you would do better in your careers – especially if you were able to read what you need to faster... and retain it better and longer.

All too many of you are parents with the same lament: 'How do I get David to do better at school? He thinks reading *The Beano* is the height of literature.'

I want briefly to take the time to address each one of the audiences for this book and discuss some of the factors particular to each of you.

## If you are a secondary school student

You should be particularly comfortable with the format of the book – its relatively short sentences and paragraphs, occasionally humorous (hopefully) headings and subheadings and the language used. I wrote it with you in mind.

It is not very helpful to work out how to study if you cannot read and retain information, so learning how to approach your reading assignments is definitely important. This will not only help with your studying now but is a key to success for your future.

## If you are a 'traditional' college or university student

Having left school and gone to college or university, I would hope that you have already learned all of the basic study techniques, especially reading and writing. If not, take the time to learn these skills now. You may have been able to deceive yourself that mediocre or even poor reading skills didn't stop you from completing, or even succeeding at secondary school. However, I guarantee you will not be able to fool anyone at college or university. You must master all of the skills in this book to survive, let alone succeed.

## If you are the parent of a student of any age

Your child's school is probably doing little if anything to teach him or her how to study, which means he or she is not learning how to learn. And that means he or she is not learning how to succeed.

What can parents do? There are probably even more dedicated parents out there than dedicated students. Here are the rules for parents of students of any age.

1 **Set up a homework area**. Free of distraction, well lit, with all necessary supplies to hand.

2 **Set up a homework routine**. When and where it gets done. Same start time every day.

3 **Set homework priorities**. Make the point that homework is the priority – before meeting friends, watching TV, etc.

4 **Make reading a habit** – for them, certainly, but also for yourselves, if it is not already. Children will inevitably do what you do, not what you say.

5 **Turn off the TV**. Or, at the very least, severely limit when and how much TV watching is appropriate – this can be the toughest rule.

6 **Talk to the teachers**. Find out what your children are supposed to be learning. If you do not, you cannot really supervise. You might be teaching them things at odds with what the teacher is trying to do.

7 **Encourage and motivate**, but do not nag them to do their homework. It does not work.

8 **Supervise their work**, but do not fall into the trap of doing their homework for them.

9 **Praise them to succeed**, but do not overpraise them for mediocre work.

10 **Convince older students of reality**. Learning and believing that the real world does not care about their marks, but measures them solely by what they know and what they can do is a lesson that will save many tears, including yours.

11 **If you can afford it, get your children a computer** and all the software they can handle. Your children, whatever their age, must master computer technology in order to survive, let alone succeed, in and after school. A recent decade-long study has shown that children who master computers learn faster and get higher exam marks.

## The importance of your involvement

Do not for a minute underestimate the importance of your commitment to your child's success: your involvement in your child's education is absolutely essential to his or her eventual success.

Surprisingly, the results of every study done over the last two decades about what affects a child's success at school clearly demonstrate that only one factor *overwhelmingly* affects it, every time – parental involvement. Not the size of the school, the money spent on each pupil, the number of language labs, how many students go on to university, or how many good teachers there are. All are factors, but none are as significant as the effect you can have.

So please, take the time to read this book. Learn what your children should be learning. You can help tremendously, even if you were not a brilliant student yourself, even if you never learned good study skills. You can learn now with your child – not only will it help him or her at school, it will also help you in your job, whatever your field.

## If you are a non-traditional student

If you are going back to further education at the age of 25, 45, 65 or 85 – you probably need the help offered in *Improve Your Reading*, and the other books in this series, more than anyone. Why? You may have been able to deceive yourself that mediocre or even poor reading skills didn't stop you from completing, perhaps even succeeding in, secondary school. I guarantee you will not be able to fool anyone at college or university. You must master all of the skills in this book to survive, let alone succeed. As much as I emphasise that it is rarely too early to learn good study habits, I must also emphasise that it is never too late.

If you are returning to education and attempting to carry even a partial course load while simultaneously holding down a job, bringing up a family, or both, there are some particular problems you face that you probably did not the first time you went to school.

### Time and money pressure

Let's face it, when all you had to worry about was going to school, it simply had to be easier than going to college or university, bringing up a family and working for a living simultaneously. Mastering all of the techniques of time management is even more essential if you are to effectively juggle your many responsibilities to your career, family, clubs, friends, etc, with your commitment to education. Money management may well be another essential skill – how to pay for child care or how to manage all your responsibilities while cutting your hours at work to make time for college.

## Self-imposed fears of inadequacy

You may well convince yourself that you are just 'out of practice' with all this college stuff. You do not even remember what to do with a highlighter. While some of this fear is valid, most is not; I suspect what many of you are really fearing is that you are not in that learning 'mentality' any more, that you do not 'think' the same way.

I think these last fears are groundless. You have been out there thinking and doing for quite a few years, perhaps very successfully, so it is ridiculous to think college or university will be so different. It will not be. Relax. You may have had a series of jobs, brought up a family, saved money, taken on more and more responsibility. Concentrate on how much more qualified you are for college now than you were then.

## Feeling you are 'out of your element'

This is a slightly different fear, the fear that you just do not fit in any more. After all, you are not 18 again, but neither are many of the students at college today. Nowadays more college and university students are older than 25 and you will probably feel more in your element now than you did the first time round.

## You will see teachers differently

It is doubtful you will have the same awe as you did the first time round. At worst, you will consider teachers your equals. At best, you will consider them younger and not necessarily as successful or experienced as you are. Either way, you probably will not be quite as ready to treat your college or university lecturers as if they were akin to God.

## There _are_ differences in academic life

It is slower than the 'real' world, and you may well be moving significantly faster than its normal pace. When you were 18, an afternoon without lessons meant meeting your friends. Now it might mean catching up on a week's worth of errands, cooking (and freezing) dinners for a week and/or writing four essays to be handed in this week. Despite your own hectic schedule, do not expect university life to accelerate in response. You will have to get used to people and systems with far less interest in speed.

## Some random thoughts about learning

Learning should not be painful and certainly does not have to be boring, although it is far too often both. However, it is not necessarily going to be wonderful and painless either. Sometimes you actually have to really apply yourself to work something out or get a project done. That is reality.

It is also reality that everything is not readily apparent or easily understandable and can cause confusion. Tell yourself that is OK and learn how to get past it. If you actually think you understand everything you have read the first time through, you are deluding yourself. Learning something slowly does not mean there is something wrong with you. It may be a subject that virtually everybody learns slowly. A good student does not panic when something does not seem to be getting through the haze. He just takes his time, follows whatever steps apply and remains confident that the penny will eventually drop.

Parents often ask me, 'How can I motivate my teenager?' My initial response is usually to smile and say, 'If I knew the answer to that question, I would have retired very wealthy quite some time ago'. However, I think there is an answer, but it is not something parents can do, it is something you, the student, have to decide: are you going to spend the school day interested and alert or bored and resentful?

It is really that simple. Why not develop the attitude that you have to go to school anyway, so rather than being bored or miserable while you are there, you might as well be active and learn as much as possible? The difference between a C and an A or B for many students is, I firmly believe, merely a matter of wanting to do better. As I constantly stress in interviews, inevitably you will leave school and, very quickly, you will discover the premium is on what you know and what you can do. Marks will not count any more, neither will exam results. So you can learn it all now or regret it later.

How many times have you said to yourself, 'I do not know why I am even trying to learn this (calculus, algebra, geometry, physics, chemistry, history, etc). I will never use this again'? Remember, you have no idea what you are going to need to know tomorrow or next week, let alone next year or in the next decade.

I have been amazed in my own life how things I did with no specific purpose in mind (except probably to earn money) turned out years later to be not just invaluable to my life or career but essential. How was I to know when I took German as my language choice in secondary school that the most important international trade show in book publishing, my field, was in Frankfurt... Germany? Or that the basic skills I learned one year working for an accountant (while I was writing my first book) would become essential when I later started four companies? Or how important basic maths skills would be in selling and negotiating over the years?

So learn it all. Do not be surprised if the subject you think is least likely ever to be useful ends up being the key to your fame and fortune.

## Do it your way

You will find a plethora of techniques, tips, tricks, gimmicks and what-have-yous, some or all of which may work for you, some of which may not. Pick and choose, change and adapt, work out what works for you, because you are the one responsible for creating your study system, not me.

Occasionally I will point out 'my way' of doing something. I may even suggest that I think it offers some clear advantages to all the alternative ways of accomplishing the same thing, but that does not mean it is carved in stone.

I have used the phrase 'Study smarter, not harder' as a sort of catch-phrase for this series of books. What does it mean to you? Does it mean I guarantee you will spend less time studying? Or that the least amount of time is best? Or that studying is not ever supposed to be hard?

Hardly. It does mean that studying inefficiently is wasting time that could be spent doing other (probably more fun) things and that getting your studying done as quickly and efficiently as possible is a realistic, worthy and attainable goal. I am no stranger to hard work, but I try not to work harder than I have to.

## In case you were wondering

Before we get on with all the tips and techniques necessary, let me make an important point about my study books.

I believe in gender equality, in writing as well as in life. Unfortunately, I find constructions such as 'he and she,' 's/he,' 'womyn' and other such combinations to be sometimes painfully awkward. I have therefore attempted to sprinkle pronouns of both genders throughout the text.

I have tried to create a system that is usable, that is useful, that is practical, that is learnable. One that you can use – whatever your age, whatever your level of achievement, whatever your IQ – to start doing better at school, at work and in life immediately.

# 1 Reading: mother of all study skills

I think you will find this is a book unlike any you have read before. So, if you take the time to read it, it will make everything else you have to read – whatever your student status, your job or your age – a lot easier to get through.

Why? Because I am going to show you how to plough through all your reading assignments – whatever the subjects – better and faster… and how to remember more of what you read.

This book is not a gimmicky speed-reading method. It is not a spelling and grammar guide. Nor is it a lecture on the joys of reading. It is a practical guide, geared to you – a student of any age who is not necessarily a poor reader, but who wants to get more from reading and do better at school and in life.

Personally, I love to read: the classics, spy thrillers, sports magazines, the newspaper, the back of the cereal box. When bored, tired, relaxing or eating, I will read anything handy, just to be able to read something.

However, just because I loved to read did not mean it was easy for me to face some of those tedious textbook reading assignments. As a student, you will inevitably be required to spend hours poring through ponderous, fact-filled, convoluted reading assignments for subjects that are required but not exactly what you would choose to put on your 'All-Time Favourites' list.

You may love reading for pleasure, but have trouble reading textbook assignments for certain subjects. You may complete the reading, but forget what you have read nearly as quickly as you read it. Or you may hate the thought of sitting still to read anything. Whatever kind of student you are – and whatever your level of reading skill – this book has been written to help you overcome your reading challenge, whatever it may be.

This also includes, for those of you who left school a long time ago, reading those sleep-inducing business tomes, trade magazine articles and other work-related stuff that is rarely reader friendly.

You will learn what you should read – and what you do not have to. You will discover how to cut down on the time you spend reading, how to identify the main idea in your reading, as well as the important details, and how to remember more of what you read.

I will show you different ways to read various types of books, from dry science texts to cumbersome classics.

Who knows? I might even convince you reading is fun.

When you are a good reader, the world is your oyster – you qualify for better colleges and universities, better jobs, better pay. Poor readers qualify for poor jobs and less fulfilling lives.

## Ready to begin? Get motivated!

Any attempt to improve your reading must begin with motivation. Reading is not a genetic trait that is written into your DNA – there is no gene that makes you a good or bad reader such as the ones that decide your hair or eye colour. For the most part, reading is an acquired skill. A skill you can grasp, grow and sharpen, but one that you have to want to attain.

In this book I will address a number of very practical techniques that will increase your reading comprehension. But they are only techniques.

You will invariably find them utterly useless if you are not motivated to read in the first place.

As one sports equipment commercial reminds us 'Just Do It!' This attitude – not technique – is where the quest for improved reading begins. You must make reading a habit.

## Good reader versus poor reader

Look at the following comparison of a good reader and a poor reader as if you were a personnel director who could hire just one of the individuals.

▌ **Good reader**: You read for purpose. You have clearly defined your reason for reading – a question you want answered, facts you must remember, ideas you need to grasp, current events that affect you or just for the pleasure of following a well-written story.

▌ **Poor reader**: Yes, you read, but often have no real reason for doing so. You aimlessly struggle through assigned reading, with little effort to grasp the 'message'.

▌ **Good reader**: You read and assimilate thought. You hear and digest the concepts and ideas communicated.

▌ **Poor reader**: You get lost in the muddle of words, struggling to make sense of what the author is trying to say. You are often bored because you force yourself to read every word to 'get the message'… which you don't.

▌ **Good reader**: You read critically and ask questions to evaluate whether the author's arguments are reasonable or off-the-wall. You recognise biases and do not just 'believe' everything you read.

▌ **Poor reader**: You swallow everything you read – hook, line and sinker. You suffer from the delusion that everything in print is true, and are easily swayed from what you formerly believed to be true by any argument that sounds good.

▌ **Good reader**. You read a variety of books, magazines and newspapers – not limiting your reading to a Tom Sharpe humour book. You enjoy all types of reading – fiction, poetry, biography, current events.

▌ **Poor reader**: You are a one-track reader – you read the sports pages, comics or Gothic novels. Current events? You catch up on world affairs from occasional TV news 'sound bites'.

▌ **Good reader**: You enjoy reading and embrace it as an essential tool in your desire to better yourself.

▮ **Poor reader**: You hate to read, deeming it a chore to be endured only when you have to. Reading is 'boring'.

Take a minute and ask yourself, who would you rather hire? Yes, you might hire Mr Poor Reader... in some low-paid job. But would you ever put someone with such low-level skills in a responsible position?

At this point, I won't ask you to evaluate your own level of reading skills. Characterising yourself as a 'good' or 'poor' reader was not the point of this exercise. What is important is to realise that Ms Good Reader did not start life reading Shakespearean sonnets and quoting Winston Churchill. She learned to read the same way you and I did – with 'Janet and John'.

In time and through making reading a habit, Ms Good Reader acquired and honed a skill that will open a world of opportunity to her.

Mr Poor Reader, at some point, decided that being a good reader was not worth the effort and made poor reading his habit. The good news is that being a poor reader is not a life sentence – you can improve your reading. The challenge is to find the motivation.

## How fast can you understand?

> When we read too fast or too slowly,
> we understand nothing.
>
> PASCAL

Are you worried that you read too slowly? You probably shouldn't be – less rapid readers are not necessarily less able. What counts is what you comprehend and remember. And like anything else, practice will probably increase your speed levels. If you must have a ranking, read the following 500-word passage on American politics from start to finish, noting the time taken on your watch. Score yourself as follows.

| | |
|---|---|
| Under 30 seconds | very fast |
| 31–45 seconds | fast |
| 46–60 seconds | high average |
| 61–89 seconds | average |
| 90–119 seconds | slow |
| 120 seconds or more | very slow |

If you are like most members of the third estate, you wonder if there are any real differences between politicians who say they're liberal Democrats and those who say they're conservative Republicans. Aren't they all just a bunch of slick-talking, vote-seeking, pocket-lining, power-hungry egomaniacs bent on getting elected?

Maybe some are, but they also tend to have basic philosophical differences guiding their slick-talking, vote-seeking, pocket-lining, power-hungry pursuit of office.

Let's look at some fundamental political, social and economic differences between these groups.

Conservatives tend to champion free enterprise, or limited governmental control of the economy. They make the argument that people should be rewarded for their hard work and shouldn't expect government hand-outs through the welfare system. They are also heavily into national defence, law enforcement and promotion of the fundamental values of family, God and country (makes you want to break out into several verses of the 'Star Spangled Banner'– doesn't it?)

Liberals take a more paternalistic view of government. It is the last and only hope for many members of society who have suffered at the unscrupulous or uncaring hands of others. They contend that business would run amok, exploiting workers and consumers in every market exchange, if not for government oversight. They also tend to be more concerned that everyone in society has equal access to a fair share of the economic pie, regardless of race, creed, sex, religion, shoe size, bank account, eye colour or planet of birth. Their hearts bleed for all.

These differences often place conservatives and liberals, Republicans and Democrats, on different sides of issues such as school prayer, environmental quality, welfare reform, worker safety, abortion, the death penalty, business regulation, sex education and, well, just about every other newsworthy topic over the past ten zillion years.

Of course, some of you might claim to be registered Democrats, yet say you support school prayer and welfare reform; or contend you're a Republican but you sure as anything want clean air and water and are willing to fight for them. Does this make you schizophrenic or hypocritical? Not necessarily. In fact, there are few truly liberal Democrats or absolutely conservative Republicans who support, without question, the 'straight' party line. Many members of the third estate have a combination of liberal and conservative views... just like you.

---

Now answer the following questions without referring back to the text. (The answers are on page 19.)

1 According to the author, which of the following do traditional Republicans *not* favour?

A  School prayer
B  Sex education
C  Welfare reform
D  Banning abortion

2 Republicans favour:

A  Limited governmental control of the economy
B  Free enterprise
C  Both
D  Neither

3 Democrats favour:

A  Less stringent environmental laws
B  Lower taxes
C  Both
D  Neither

4 The author is probably:

   A   A Democrat
   B   A Republican
   C   An independent
   D   A smart aleck

A good reader should be reading fast or very fast and have answered at least three of the four questions correctly.

You should only worry – and plan to do something about it – if you fall in the slow or very slow range and/or missed two or more questions. Otherwise, you are probably reading as fast as you need to and retaining most of what you read.

Again, the relationship between speed and comprehension is all important: read too fast and you may comprehend *less*; reading more slowly does not necessarily mean you are not grasping the material.

## What decreases reading speed/comprehension?

1 Reading aloud or moving your lips when you read.

2 Reading mechanically – using your finger to follow words, moving your head as you read.

3 Applying the wrong kind of reading to the material.

4 Lacking sufficient vocabulary.

There are several things you can do to improve these reading mechanics.

## To increase your reading speed

1 Focus your attention and concentration.

2 Eliminate outside distractions.

3 Provide for an uncluttered, comfortable environment.

4 Do not get stuck on single words or sentences, but do look up (in the dictionary) key words that you must understand in order to grasp an entire concept.

5 Try to grasp overall concepts rather than attempting to understand every detail.

6 If you find yourself moving your lips when you read (vocalisation), practise reading with a pen or some other (non-toxic, non-sugary) object in your mouth. If it falls out while you are reading, you know you have to keep working.

## To increase comprehension

1 Try to make the act of learning sequential – comprehension is built by adding new knowledge to existing knowledge.

2 Review and rethink at designated points in your reading. Test yourself to see if the importance of the material is getting through.

3 If things do not add up, discard your conclusions. Go back, reread and try to find an alternative conclusion.

4 Summarise what you have read, rephrasing it in your notes, in your own words.

Most importantly, read at the speed that is comfortable for you. Although I can read extremely fast, I choose to read novels much more slowly so I can appreciate the author's word play. Similarly, any material that I find particularly difficult to grasp slows me down completely. I read newspapers, popular magazines, etc very fast, seeking to grasp the information but not worrying about every detail.

Should you take some sort of speed reading course, especially if your current speed level is low?

Reading for speed has some merit – many people who are slow readers read as little as possible, simply because they find it so tedious and boring. But just reading faster is not the answer to becoming a good reader.

I cannot see that such a course could particularly harm you in any way. I can also, however, recommend that you simply keep practising reading, which will increase your speed naturally.

## Don't remember less... faster

Retention is primarily a product of what you understand. It has little to do with how fast you read, how good an outline you can construct or how many fluorescent colours you can highlight with in your textbooks. Reading a text, grasping the message and remembering it, are the fundamentals that make for high-level retention. Reading at a 1,000-word-per-minute jog does not necessarily mean that you have any idea what a text really says.

As you work towards improving your reading, realise that speed is secondary to comprehension. If you can read an assignment faster than anyone in the classroom, but cannot give a one-sentence synopsis of what you read, you lose. If you really get the author's message – even if it takes you an hour or two longer than some of your friends – your time will pay off in huge dividends now and later in life.

That is why this book concentrates only on how you as a student can increase what you retain from your reading assignments. Whether you are reading a convoluted textbook that bores even the tutor to tears, or a magazine article, newspaper feature or novel, you follow a certain process to absorb what you have read, which consists of:

1 Grasping the main idea.

2 Gathering the facts.

3 Working out the sequence of events.

4 Drawing conclusions.

When you spend an hour reading an assignment, then cannot recall what you have just read, it is usually because a link in this chain has been broken. You have missed one of these crucial steps in your reading process, leaving your understanding of the material filled with gaps.

To increase your retention rate, you need to master each level in this chain of comprehension. Not everything you read will require understanding on all four levels. Following a set of cooking instructions, for example, simply requires you to perceive the sequence for adding all the ingredients. Other reading will demand that you are able to compile facts, identify a thesis and give some critical thought as to its validity.

Ms Good Reader is not only able to perform at each level of comprehension, but also has developed an instinct. She recognises that certain things she reads can be read just to gather facts or just to grasp the main idea. She is then able to read quickly to accomplish this goal and move on to her next assignment – or to that Steven King novel she has been longing to read.

This book will help you develop a sense of what is involved in each step of the reading process.

The first chapters will address these different steps and provide exercises designed to help you master each stage in the process of retaining what you read.

In the final chapters, we will look at how to read literature, how to read a maths or science textbook and how to outline so that you can easily review a text.

By the time you finish this short book, you should find that by following the procedures suggested, you have significantly improved your reading comprehension.

## Finding other textbooks

Few textbooks are written by what most of us would even remotely call professional writers. While the authors and editors may well be experts, even legends, in a particular subject, writing in jargon-free, easy-to-grasp-prose is probably not their strong point. You will occasionally be assigned a textbook that is so obtuse you are not even sure whether to read it from front to back, upside down or inside out.

If you find a particular chapter, section or entire textbook as tough to read as getting your baby brother to do you a favour, go to the library or the bookshop and find another book covering the same subject area that you can understand. You could even consider asking your teacher or professor for recommendations. He or she will probably make your job of finding a readable text a lot easier. You may even score some brownie points for your apparent initiative (as long as you do not wonder aloud what caused him or her to select that torturous text in the first place).

'Ron,' I hear you grumbling, 'what happened to the "study smarter, not harder" bit? This can't possibly be a time saver. I bet the books don't even cover the subject in the same way, let alone follow the same sequence – I'll be stuck slogging through two books.'

All true, possibly. But if you just don't get it, perhaps it is because the author does not know how to explain it. Maybe it is not your fault. Too many students have sweated, moaned, dropped out of classes, even changed degree course because they thought they were dumb, when it is possible it is the wretched textbook that is dense, not you. So instead of continuing to slog though the mire, find an expert who can actually write – they are out there – and learn what you need to. After finally understanding the subject by reading this other text, you will find much of the original textbook much easier to use... presuming you need it at all.

Answers to quiz: B, C, D, D.

# 2 Reading with purpose

Even if you consider yourself 'not much of a reader', you read *something* each and every day. A magazine article, instructions for connecting up the VCR, telephone messages attached to the 'fridge, notes from the latest 'love in your life'.

Regardless of what you are reading, you have a purpose that dictates how you are going to read it – and you read different items in different ways. You would not read the VCR instructions as you would a novel, any more than you would read the magazine article in the same way as a shopping list. Without a purpose, you would find yourself reading aimlessly and very inefficiently.

Unfortunately, many of the students I have talked to have not yet realised the importance of having a purpose for reading. Their lack of reading purpose can be summed up by the proverb, 'If you aim at nothing, you will hit the bull's-eye every time'.

Before you can understand what you are reading – and remember it – you must know why you are reading it in the first place.

## Defining your purpose for reading

What is your purpose in reading? If the best answer you can come up with is, 'Because my teacher said so', you need to think again. Reading a chapter just so you can say, 'I completed my assignment', is relatively futile. You may as well put the book under your pillow and hope to absorb it by osmosis.

Unless you identify some purpose to read, you will find yourself turning the pages of your textbooks while seldom retaining anything more than the chapter titles.

According to reading experts, there are six fundamental purposes for reading.

1  To grasp a certain message.

2  To find important details.

3  To answer a specific question.

4  To evaluate what you are reading.

5  To apply what you are reading.

6  To be entertained.

Because reading with purpose is the first step towards improved comprehension, let me suggest some simple techniques you can use to identify a purpose for your textbook reading.

## Find the clues in every book

There is a group of special sections found in nearly all textbooks and technical materials (in fact, in most books except novels) that contain a wealth of information and can help you glean more from your reading. Becoming familiar with this data will enrich your reading experience and often make it easier. The following is what to look for.

▌ The first page after the title page is usually the *table of contents* – a chapter-by-chapter list of the book's contents. Some are surprisingly detailed, listing every major point or topic covered in each chapter.

▌ The first prose section (after the title page, table of contents and, perhaps, *acknowledgements page*, in which the author thanks other authors, his editor, researcher, friends, relatives, teachers, etc, most of which you can ignore), the *preface*, is usually a description of what information you will find in the book. Authors may also use the preface to point out unique aspects of their books.

▌ The *introduction* may be in place of or in addition to the preface and may be written by the author or some 'name' the author has recruited to lend additional prestige to his or her work. Most introductions are an even more detailed overview of the book – chapter-by-chapter summaries are often included to give the reader a feel for the material to be covered.

▌ *Footnotes* may be found throughout the text (a slightly elevated number following a sentence, quotation etc, eg, jim-dandy[24]) and either explained at the bottom of the page on which they appear or in a special section at the end of the text. Footnotes may be used to cite sources of direct quotes or ideas and/or to further explain a point, or add information, outside of the text. You may make it a habit to search for sources cited for further reading.

▌ If a text tends to use an alarmingly high number of terms with which you may not be familiar, the considerate author will include a *glossary* – essentially an abridged dictionary that defines all these terms.

▌ The *bibliography*, usually at the end of the book, may include the source material the author used to research the textbook, a list of recommended reading, or both. It is usually organised alphabetically by author.

▌ *Appendices* containing supplementary data or examples relating to subject matter covered in the text may also appear at the back of the book.

▌ The last thing in a book is usually the *index*, an alphabetical listing that references, by page number, every mention of a particular name, subject, topic, etc, in the text.

Making it a habit to utilise all of these tools in your textbook can only make your studying easier.

## Look for the clues in each chapter

Every textbook offers some clues that will help you define a purpose for reading. Begin with a very quick overview of the assignment, looking for questions that you would like answered. Consider the following elements of your reading assignment before you begin your reading.

Much as the headlines of a newspaper give you an idea of what the story is about, these elements will give insight into what the section or chapter is trying to communicate.

### *Chapter heads and subheads*

Chapter titles and bold typeface subheads announce the detail about the main topic. And, in some textbooks, paragraph headings or bold typeface 'lead-ins' announce that the author is about to provide finer details.

So start each reading assignment by going through the chapter, from beginning to end, reading only the bold typeface heads and subheads.

For example, suppose you encountered the heading, 'The Demise of the American Indian', in your history text. You might use it to form the following questions:

A    What caused the demise of the American Indian?

B    Who caused it?

C    When did it occur?

D    Why did it occur?

As you read the chapter, you will find yourself looking for the answers to these questions. You now have a purpose.

Often you may find headings that contain words or terms you do not recognise. Trying to define these terms or explain a concept should then define your purpose.

This process of headline reading takes only a few minutes, but it lays the groundwork for a more intelligent and efficient reading of the chapter. You will have some idea where the author is heading, which will give you a greater sense of what the most important details are and clarify where you should be concentrating your studying.

### End-of-chapter summaries

If you read a mystery from start to finish, the way the author hopes you will, you are likely to get thrown off the scent by 'red herrings' and other common detective novel devices. However, if you read the last page first, knowing the outcome will help you detect how the author constructed the novel and built an open-and-shut case for his or her master sleuth. You would perceive a wealth of details about the eventually un-masked murderer that might have gone unnoticed had he been just another of the leading suspects.

Similarly, knowing what the author is aiming at in a textbook will help you look for the important building blocks for his conclusions while you are reading.

It may not be fun to read a mystery novel this way, but when it comes to textbook reading, it will help you define your purpose for reading. Furthermore, it will transform you into a much more active reader, making it less likely you will doze off while being bored by the usual ponderous prose.

### Pictures, graphs and charts

Most textbooks, particularly those for science subjects, will have charts, graphs, numerical tables, maps and other illustrations. All too many students see these as fillers – padding to glance at quickly and, just as quickly, forget.

If you are giving these charts and graphs short shrift, you are really short-changing yourself. Make sure you observe how they supplement the text and what points they emphasise, and make a note of these.

### Highlighted terms, vocabulary and other facts

In some textbooks, you will discover that key terms and information are highlighted within the body text. (I don't mean highlighted by a previous student – consider such yellow-marked passages with caution.) To find the definitions of these terms, or to find the application of facts, may then be your purpose for reading.

### Questions

Some textbook publishers use a format in which key points are emphasised by questions, either within the body or at the end of the chapter. If you read these questions before reading the chapter, you will have a better idea of what material you need to pay closer attention to.

### Prereading your assignment

If you begin your reading assignment by seeking out these heads, subheads and other purpose-finding elements of the chapter, you will have completed your prereading step. What is prereading? It is simply beginning your assigned reading by reviewing these clues and defining your purpose (or purposes) for reading.

I suggest that you always preread every assignment. Why? Have you ever spent the better part of an evening ploughing through an assignment only to end up with little or no understanding of what you have just read? If the answer is yes, then you probably failed to preread it.

## Reading faster without speed reading

While the heads, subheads, first sentences and other author-provided hints we have discussed will help you get a rough idea of what a chapter is about, some of the words in that chapter will help you concentrate on the important points and ignore the unimportant. Knowing when to speed up, slow down, ignore or really concentrate will help you read both faster and more effectively.

When you see words such as 'likewise', 'in addition', 'moreover' or 'furthermore', you should realise nothing new is being introduced. If you already know what is going on, speed up or skip what is coming entirely.

On the other hand, when you see words such as 'on the other hand', 'nevertheless', 'however', 'rather' or 'but', slow down – you are getting information that adds a new perspective or contradicts what you have just read. Lastly, watch out for 'pay-off' words such as 'to summarise', 'in conclusion', 'therefore', 'consequently', 'thus' – especially if you only have time to 'hit the high points' of a chapter or you are reviewing for an exam. This is where the real nub is, where everything that went before is now presented, and this avoids having to reread the entire chapter.

## Purpose defines reading method

Typically, your purpose for reading dictates how you read. There are basically three types of reading we all do.

1 **Quick reference reading** focuses on seeking specific information that addresses a particular question or concern we might have.

2 **Critical reading** involves discerning ideas and concepts that require a thorough analysis.

3 **Aesthetic or pleasure reading** is what we do for sheer entertainment or to appreciate an author's style and ability.

As you define your purpose for reading, you will determine which method of reading is necessary to accomplish this purpose. In the following table there are some examples of types of reading, why you might read them and the method you should use.

| Type | Purpose | Method |
|------|---------|--------|
| Newspaper advertisement | To locate best price for car | Quick reference |
| Magazine | To keep abreast of current events | Quick reference |
| Self-help book | To learn to get along better with your family | Critical |
| Biology text | To prepare for an exam | Critical |
| New issue of your favourite fanzine | To take your mind off biology! | Pleasure |

If you are a good reader or want to become one, you will always fit your reading method to your reading purpose; you have trained or are training yourself in a variety of reading skills; you have no problem switching your method to accommodate your purpose; and you are unsatisfied reading only one type of material.

A poor reader, on the other hand, reads everything the same way – doggedly ploughing through the biology assignment, the newspaper and the Stephen King novel… word by painful word. Reading with purpose is both foreign and worrying to such a person, which makes it difficult for him or her to adapt a method of reading.

## Become an active reader

Reading with purpose is as vital to your comprehension and retention as oxygen is to life. It is the cornerstone of active reading, reading that involves thinking – that process of engaging your mind and emotions in what the author is trying to communicate. Too many readers try to absorb information passively as their eyes move across the page. The active reader involves him- or herself in receiving a message – a fact, an idea, an opinion – that is readily retained because he or she has a purpose.

The following is a passage adapted from *Make the Most of Your Workday* by Jonathan and Susan Clark (Career Press, 1994). Preread the passage in order to determine a purpose for reading. Use page 32 as your note page to jot down questions that may have been raised through your preread, and the purpose.

---

### Are you really trying to do too much?

We all need checks and balances to manage life's resources and responsibilities, and that's what this chapter is all about. You may be overloaded with responsibilities and demands. You may feel incapable of effectively organising and managing all of your projects. You may be hoping for a mixture of ideas and solutions that, blended together, can restore a feeling of control.

It's possible that all your concerns about your time boil down to one simple fact: you may simply be trying to do too much.

The best-organised schedule, the most well-planned 'daily action plan', the most effectively applied list of 10 steps or 12 ideas, cannot change your situation if you are trying to accomplish more than you have time to do.

How can you determine whether self-overload conditions already exist? What can you do to change those conditions? Generally speaking, if you feel overloaded, you are overloaded. If you don't feel that you are presently overloaded, you may fear that you're heading that way… fast. Your question then is, 'How can I keep this from happening?'

Whether you've already reached the breaking point or see the point approaching fast, to avoid certain demise you must take a long, hard look at all of your commitments and activities. You must be honest and realistic. The very first step is to ask yourself, 'If I were not already doing this, would I choose to get involved?'

## A case study

Jim North, a personnel director of a small manufacturing firm, began attending monthly meetings of a local organisation of personnel directors.

Although Jim enjoyed the association with other professionals in his field, he found it difficult to attend the breakfasts every month. He frequently got his most productive work done early in the day, and sometimes the meetings seemed to have only marginal professional benefits, since a number of the members seemed mainly interested in the meeting as a social occasion.

Jim was surprised when Gerry Duckworth, a member he knew only casually, called one day and asked if he would consider running for vice-president of the organisation for the coming year. When Jim asked what the position involved, Gerry said, 'Oh, you really don't have to do anything. We just need someone to hold that office'.

As it turned out, Jim was the only person nominated, and he was elected to the office.

A few days later, Kathy Cornell, the president, called Jim and told him there was a lunch meeting scheduled later that week for all the officers of the organisation.

When Jim went to the officers' meeting, he discovered that the vice-president had numerous responsibilities, including planning the programmes for the breakfasts each month and heading up the annual new members campaign. Kathy excitedly told the group that she had just learned her company was sending her across the country for three months to oversee the opening of a new office. This meant Jim would function as president for that time.

Jim obviously realised this new job was a lot bigger than he had been told it was. If he had known it entailed so much responsibility, he probably would have declined the nomination. He began to envision the additional hours and energy required (which he really didn't have) to serve an organisation of questionable value to him, and felt overwhelmed. He also found himself feeling resentful that the importance of the job had been misrepresented to him. What was Jim's biggest mistake? If you were Jim, what would you do now?

## What actually happened

Jim quickly reassessed his own priorities and determined that this new responsibility did not fit into them. He analysed what impact giving up that much additional time and energy would have on the activities to which he had already committed. He wondered how much he could do in a new area if he were to continue to direct the same time and energy to his priorities.

At the end of the meeting, he asked Kathy to stay for a few minutes. Then he told her, 'Kathy, if I had realised the scope of this job, I never would have agreed to serve. I am sorry I didn't ask more questions when Gerry called, and I realise this will put the association in a temporary bind, but I am going to have to resign from the office'.

Kathy reluctantly accepted Jim's resignation. She appointed another vice-president before the next meeting and made the announcement in the organisation's news-letter.

For a few months, Jim felt a little uncomfortable at the meetings. A few people teased him about 'chickening out' of the job, but the teasing eventually stopped. When the election of officers came around the next year, Jim reflected gratefully on his decision, realising he had been wise to put his efforts into his priorities.

## What it all meant to Jim

Jim could have decided to make the best of his position and plan great programmes and spearhead an enthusiastic new members campaign. Maybe he would have got even more out of the meetings and his opportunities to network with the other members of the organisation.

But sometimes people simply spread themselves too thinly – trying to do too much and please too many people. When you identify your priorities by asking, 'What's important to me?' it is often far more satisfying and rewarding to redirect additional time and effort to previous commitments than to add even more activities to an already jammed calendar.

## And what it means to you

Put yourself in this story. Change the situation to one you are facing. Wouldn't you really rather be out from under this responsibility than trying to juggle it and fit it in with other, more important matters? Won't you feel good when that commitment is no longer on your list?

Remember, for any project that you're already involved in or are thinking about taking on, ask yourself this question, 'Can I make a strong personal commitment to invest my time and abilities in this purpose, project or pursuit?' If the answer is 'I can't make a full commitment', then it's best not to start it or, if already involved, to find a way out.

# Your notes

What clues can you find that help you define a purpose for reading this passage?

_____

_____

_____

_____

What purpose or purposes did you determine for reading this passage?

_____

_____

_____

_____

What method, based on your purpose, would you use to read this passage?

_____

_____

_____

_____

# 3 *Finding the main idea*

In all good writing, there is a controlling thesis or message that connects all the specific details and facts together. This concept or idea is usually expressed as a generalisation that summarises the entire text.

Good comprehension results when you are able to grasp this main message, even if you sometimes forget some of the details. When you understand the intent, you have a context in which to evaluate the reasoning, the attitude and whether the evidence cited really is supportive of the conclusions drawn.

An obsession for facts can obscure the 'big picture', giving you an understanding of the trees but no concept of the forest. How many of you have spent hours studying for an important exam, collecting dates, names, terms and formulas, but failed to ferret out the main idea, the underlying concept that is composed of these facts?

In longer, more involved readings, many messages are combined to form a chain of thought, which, in turn, may or may not be communicating one thesis or idea.

Your ability to capture this chain of thought determines your level of comprehension – and what you retain.

## Dissecting your reading assignment

To succeed in identifying the main idea in any reading assignment, you must learn to use these helpful tools.

1 The topic sentence of a paragraph.

2 Summary sentences.

3 Supporting sentences.

4 Transitional statements.

As you learn to dissect your reading assignment paragraph by paragraph, identifying its many parts and their functions, you will grasp the main idea much more quickly – and remember it much longer.

## Recognising a topic sentence

Every paragraph has a topic sentence – the sentence that summarises what the paragraph is about. Even if a paragraph does not have such a clearly stated sentence, it can be implied or inferred from what is written.

Generally, the topic sentence is the first or last sentence of a paragraph – the one statement that announces, 'This is what this paragraph is all about'.

When the topic sentence is obscured or hidden, you may need to utilise two simple exercises to uncover it.

1 Pretend you are a headline writer for your local newspaper – write a headline for the paragraph you have just read.

2 Write a five-word summary describing what the paragraph is about.

### Exercise: identifying a topic sentence

Write a headline or five-word summary for each of the following paragraphs.

It is very exciting to wander through display homes or visit open houses and dream of moving in. Just remember to treat home buying or selling very seriously and take time for a reality check now and then. This is a decision you will live with for many years. 'Home'-work is the key. Knowing the finances ahead of time and setting your limits will definitely pay off.

More than ever, we are looking for meaning, fulfilment and personal growth in our lives. And we are demanding those qualities in our jobs and business as well. An organisation that understands this tends to have a happier and more productive workforce. If an organisation has a clearly articulated statement of philosophy and values, there can be a meshing of corporate and personal goals known as alignment.

◆ I ◆ I ◆ I ◆

Like it or not, government is with us and will be for a long time to come. One cannot even imagine a society that would not involve some sort of government. In that numerous needs-satisfying goods are produced only by the government, we have no choice but to keep it around. And because we have it, we have to pay taxes. The question then is whether our taxes are spent wisely. No. They are not and they never will be, because government is incredibly inefficient and incompetent. The problem is, if the government does not perform duties badly, they probably will not be performed at all.

As you can see from these three paragraphs, the topic sentence is not always clearly stated. This is also true in a number of the convoluted textbooks we all have to read. When trying to discern the main idea of such writing, you may need a more in-depth analysis.

You can begin your analysis by turning, once again, to our helpful questions. Is the passage written to address one of the questions?

1 **Who?** The paragraph focuses on a particular person or group of people. The topic sentence tells you *who* this is.

2 **When?** The paragraph is primarily concerned with *time*. The topic sentence may even begin with the word 'when'.

3 **Where**? The paragraph is oriented around a particular place or location. The topic sentence states *where* you are reading about.

4 **Why**? A paragraph that states reasons for some belief or happening usually addresses this question. The topic sentence answers *why* something is true or *why* an event happened.

5 **How**? A paragraph that identifies the way something works or the means by which something is done. The topic sentence explains the *how* of what is described.

You will notice that I did not include the question 'What?' in this list. This is not an oversight. 'What?' addresses such a broad range of possibilities that asking this question will not necessarily lead you to the topic sentence.

The best test to determine whether you have identified the topic sentence is to rephrase it as a question. If the paragraph answers the question that you have framed, you have found the topic sentence.

## Summary, support or transitional?

Another technique that will lead you to the topic sentence is to identify what purpose other sentences in the paragraph serve – a sort of process of elimination.

Generally, sentences can be characterised as summary, support or transitional.

■ **Summary sentences** state a general idea or concept. As a rule, a topic sentence is a summary sentence – a concise yet inclusive statement that expresses the general intent of the paragraph. (By definition, the topic sentence is never a support sentence.)

■ **Support sentences** provide the specific details and facts that give credibility to the author's points of view. They give examples, explain arguments, offer evidence or attempt to prove something as true or false. They are not meant to state generally what the author wants to communicate – they are intended to be specific, not conceptual, in nature.

**Transitional sentences** move the author from one point to another. They may be viewed as bridges connecting the paragraphs in a text, suggesting the relationship between what you have just read and what you are about to read. Good readers are attuned to the signals such sentences provide – they are buzzers that shout out, 'This is what you are going to find out next'.

Transitional sentences may also alert you to what you should just have learned. Unlike support sentences, transitional sentences provide invaluable and direct clues to identifying the topic sentence.

## Some examples of transitional signals

Any sentence that continues a progression of thought or succession of concepts is a transitional sentence. Such a sentence may begin with a word such as 'first', 'next', 'finally' or 'then' and indicate the before or after connection between changes, improvements or alterations.

Transitional sentences that begin in this way should raise the following questions in your mind.

1 Do I know what the previous examples were?

2 What additional example am I about to learn?

3 What was the situation prior to the change?

Other transition statements suggest a change in argument, thought or an exception to a rule. These will generally be introduced by words such as 'but', 'although', 'though', 'rather', 'however' or similar conjunctions that suggest an opposing thought.

Such words should raise these questions.

1 What is the gist of the argument I just read?

2 What will the argument I am about to read state?

3 To what rule is the author offering an exception?

In your effort to improve your reading, developing the ability to recognise the contrast between general, inclusive words and statements (summary sentences) and specific, detail-oriented sentences (transitional or support sentences) is paramount.

## Taking notes

The final step towards grasping and retaining the main idea of any paragraph is taking notes. There are several traditional methods students employ – outlining, highlighting, mapping and drawing concept trees.

Whichever method you employ to retain the main idea, focus on the topic sentences, not on the specific details.

If you are a highlighter – you enjoy colouring textbooks with fluorescent markers – you will want to assign one colour that you will always use to highlight topic sentences. Avoid what too many students do – highlighting virtually every paragraph. This practice will only extend your review time – you will find yourself rereading instead of reviewing.

If you use outlining or mapping techniques (diagramming what you read rather than spending time worrying about Roman numerals and whether to use lower case letters or upper case letters on certain lines) you will find that your time will be best spent writing five-word summaries of the topic sentences.

If you find yourself getting bogged down in details and specifics, you are wasting valuable time. Again, writers are using these details to communicate their concepts – they are not necessarily to be remembered.

Read the following passage from *Economic Literacy* by Orley M Amos, Jr (Career Press, 1994), looking for the topic sentences. Then summarise the main idea or ideas in five-word phrases.

## An altogether look at unions

Unions are organisations of workers – in the same industry, working for the same company, or in the same occupation – that negotiate with their employers over things like wages, fringe benefits, working conditions, hiring and firing procedures and other job-related items. The formal negotiation, where the union and the company seek to work out a contractual agreement on these various issues, is termed collective bargaining.

In recent years, most of these collective bargaining agreements have been pretty straightforward. Unions demand a few things, companies return with their 'best' offers, then they haggle back and forth until they reach a compromise. If this sounds a lot like buying a car or house, it is. It is the same sort of one-on-one negotiation that takes place in many markets.

While the sorts of things that unions and management do to each other might appear childish, they have a serious and violent history. Their confrontations are as fundamental as the differences between the second and third estates. We can find the seeds of their conflicts growing out of our economy's transition from the simple fabrication methods of blacksmiths, carpenters and other mediaeval craftsmen to the large factories that marked the onset of the industrial revolution.

In the early years of the industrial revolution, with hundreds or even thousands of workers in a single factory, the balance of market control was tipped to the side of the second estate. The handful of employers were pretty much able to dictate wages and working conditions.

Workers had about the same status as felled trees, molten steel or railroad cars filled with slaughterhouse-bound cattle. Wages were extremely low and working conditions were, at best, downright deadly. That is when unions came on the scene.

Battles between the new unions and the fat cat employers often turned bloody. Companies did not hesitate to use force

– armed security guards and government soldiers – on the rabble-rousers. The unions fought back with an assortment of their own guerrilla tactics. Most of the violence ended with laws and court cases in the 1930s that forged a set of collective bargaining rules.

Try again with this brief excerpt from, 'A National Care Agenda', by Suzanne Gordon, which appeared in the January 1991 edition of *The Atlantic Monthly*.

The United States is experiencing an extreme crisis in caring. As a society we cannot seem to muster the political will to care for the most precious things we produce: other human beings.

The United Sates has slipped to 25th place in the world in its infant-mortality rate. Twenty per cent of America's children are destitute. More then 37 million people have no health insurance; 20 million to 30 million more are underinsured. Today, as patients are discharged earlier and earlier from the nation's hospitals, family members are increasingly asked to provide for their complex medical and emotional needs.

It is estimated that 1.8 million women care for children and elders simultaneously, and 33 per cent of women do so in addition to holding down jobs.

Yet not only do these care givers, who relieve our health-care system of a tremendous financial burden, receive little help; they are often penalised for providing such care, through the loss of wages or of the job itself.

The author is throwing around a lot of statistics to impress upon her readers that the United States must give some consideration to people who provide infants and older people with home health care. Should we remember the statistics about infant mortality, inadequate health insurance, the burdens on working women? Should these statistics appear in our notes?

If we read linearly, starting at the beginning and plodding along to the last word, we probably would be tempted to write down these numbers and what they mean in our notes. But, if we were to look ahead in the article (and glance at the sub-heads), we would find that the author is actually making a case for investments in home care by the federal government and talking about where the money should come from.

Therefore, the statistics are not especially important, but the enormity of the problem to which they give credence is.

I did not always keep my summaries to five words, but I distilled the main ideas to the fewest words that I could.

Neither did I always write one summary statement per paragraph – just what was needed to capture the main idea or ideas from each paragraph.

# 4 *Gathering the facts*

> *Now, what I want is Facts. Teach these boys and girls nothing but Facts. Facts alone are wanted in life. Plant nothing else, and root out everything else. You can only form the minds of reasoning animals upon Facts. Nothing else will ever be of any service to them. This is the principle on which I bring up my own children, and this is the principle on which I bring up these children. Stick to Facts, sir!*

> CHARLES DICKENS, *Hard Times*

Seeking out the facts, as Dickens's character encourages us to do, is also an effective way to confront your classroom reading assignments.

A 'just the facts, ma'am' approach is not the whole formula for scholastic success, but you will find that most of your assigned reading needs a thorough recall of the facts.

In the previous chapter, we discussed the 'forest' – the main idea. In this chapter, we will concentrate on 'the trees' – how to read to gather facts, the specific details that support and develop the author's main point.

## Facts: building blocks for ideas

Facts are the building blocks that give credibility to concepts and ideas. Your ability to gather and assimilate these facts will dramatically enhance your success at remembering what the author wanted to communicate.

If, however, you spend so much time studying the trees that you lose sight of the forest, your reading effectiveness will be limited. You must learn to discern which facts are salient to your understanding, and which ones to leave for the next Trivial Pursuit update.

If you are trying to identify your purpose for reading this chapter, it is threefold:

1 To develop the skill of scanning a text for facts as quickly as possible.

2 To distinguish between an important detail and a trivial one.

3 To learn how to skim text – reading and absorbing its essence, even when you are not looking for anything in particular.

## Deciphering the message

The author of any kind of writing should have something to say, a message to communicate.

Unfortunately, such messages are often lost in the excess of words many authors use to 'dress up' their basic point. It is your job to rake through the mess and get to the heart of the text.

You need to approach each reading assignment with the mindset of a detective. There is a mystery to be solved, and you are the master investigator. The goal is to work out what the text is trying to communicate – regardless of how deeply it is buried in the quagmire of convoluted language.

### What is the message?

The first step in any good investigation is to collect all of the clues. What are the facts? By spending a few minutes of your time discerning these concrete facts, you will be far better equipped to digest what it is the author is trying to communicate.

But how do you extract the facts when they appear to be hidden in an impenetrable forest of words? You may need a little help – from 'who-what-when-where-why-and-how'. It seems that the facts readily come to the fore when these six trusty questions are called upon the scene.

**Exercise**: Read the following passage, keeping these six words in mind. After you have finished reading it, answer the questions that follow. Be careful – you may have to slow down a bit.

As Boris Yeltsin seeks to overcome an approval rating that hasn't reached double digits in months and confound countrymen who have declared he has no chance in the June elections, the Communists, sensing a chance for victory in a popular election, have suddenly become courteous and willing to compromise. Since they already dominate the newly elected Parliament, their aim seems to be to keep the other political parties fighting among themselves, giving them little reason or excuse for establishing an anti-Communist coalition.

Gennadi Seleznyov, Speaker of the Parliament's lower house, or Duma, and a former editor of *Pravda*, looks more like a German banker than an old-style Communist Party apparatchik. That and his poise were two of the reasons he won out over former Central Committee member Valentin Kuptsov in the bid to become spokesperson for the 'new and improved' Russian Communists, though the fight was prolonged and nasty.

And the new Speaker has his share of enemies, among them the ultra-nationalist Vladimir Zhirnovsky, who backed the candidate of the nationalist Our Home is Russia centrist party, Ivan Rybkin, in a bid to deny the powerful position to Seleznyov. While repeatedly calling for Yeltsin's resignation, Zhirnovsky has nevertheless supported the perhaps lame duck President on many fronts, including the invasion of Chechnya, the only party in Parliament to do so.

Luckily for Seleznyov, Grigory A Yavlinsky, the liberal economist who leads Yablonko, the most reformist party in opposition to Yeltsin, refused to go along with Our Home is Russia and, by extension, Zhirnovsky. By withholding his votes, he assured Seleznyov's victory. While he maintained that he held out because he was anti-Communist, it was rumoured that he had cut a deal for a couple of much-sought-after committee posts as the price of his votes.

All of this bitter infighting suggests that Seleznyov's gamble might just pay off – it is unlikely that an anti-Communist front will emerge in time for the elections. In addition, the results of the last election must leave him sanguine. Although his party won 149 votes, more than any other (Mr Zhirinovsky's party was in second place, with 51), in reality the Communists are only a few votes shy of the 226 needed for an outright majority. It turns out that many of the 225 'independent' candidates who ran successfully were not as independent as they had declared – nearly one-third of them can be counted on to support Seleznyov's programmes.

Such control, unfortunately, tends to indicate that the new Duma will be far less flamboyant and much duller than the old, though undoubtedly more disciplined. Unlike the Speaker, many of the new Communist deputies are old-time apparatchiks who are quite accustomed to towing the party line and far less anxious to indulge in free speech.

---

1 The liberal economist who leads Yablonko is:

A   Vladimir Zhirnovsky.
B   Boris Yeltsin.
C   Grigory A Yavlinsky.
D   Ivan Rybkin.
E   Valentin Kuptsov.

2 Which of these ideas is *not* suggested in the passage?

A   Vladimir Zhirnovsky is an ultra-nationalist.
B   The Parliament's lower house is also known as the Duma.
C   Ivan Rybkin was the candidate of the Our Home is Russia centrist party.
D   Boris Yeltsin has had a high approval rating throughout the past few months.
E   Yablonko is the most reformist party in opposition to Yeltsin.

3 How many votes are needed for an outright majority?

    A  225.
    B  226.
    C  51.
    D  149.
    E  None of the above.

4 The main purpose of this passage is to explain:

    A  The history of Communism.
    B  The lifestyle of Ivan Rybkin.
    C  The odds of the June election are in favour of the
       Communist party.
    D  The fight for the Speakership.
    E  The old and new Duma.

5 Using the context of the passage, how would 'apparatchiks'
  best be described?

    A  Radical.
    B  Bold.
    C  Pioneering.
    D  Inexperienced.
    E  Traditional.

In the preceding exercise, you should have quickly read
through the text and been able to answer all five questions. If
it took you more than three minutes to do so, you spent too
much time. You were reading only to answer our six questions
– 'who?', 'what?', 'when?', 'where?', 'why?' and 'how?' Your
purpose was to get to the facts, nothing more.

## Scanning, skimming, reading, remembering

Almost everyone I know confuses *skim* and *scan*. Let me set
the record straight. *Skim is to read quickly and superficially. Scan
is to read carefully but for a specific item.* So when you *skim* a
reading passage, you are reading it in its entirety, although
you are only taking in the 'highlights'.

When you *scan* a selection, you are reading it in detail but only until you find what you are looking for. Scanning is the technique we all employ when using the phone book – unless, of course, you are in the habit of reading every name in the book to find the one you are looking for. When you scan, your eyes do not look at every word, read every sentence or think about every paragraph. Instead, they rapidly move across the page to find what you are looking for and then read that carefully.

Scanning is the fastest reading rate of all – although you are reading in detail, you are *not* seeking to comprehend or remember anything that you see until you find the bit of information you are looking for.

When I was at college, I would begin any assignment by reading the first sentence of every paragraph and by trying to answer the questions at the end of the chapter. If this did not give me a pretty good idea of the content and important details of that chapter, then – and only then – would I read it more thoroughly.

I am sure this method of skimming for the facts saved me countless hours of time (and boredom).

## Ask first, then look

When skimming for detail, you will often have a particular question, date or fact to find. You should approach the text in the same way as you would a dictionary – knowing the word, you just skim the pages to find its definition. If you must answer a specific question or read about a historic figure, you simply find a source – book, magazine or encyclopaedia – and quickly skim the text for the answer or person.

You are probably assigned a lot of reading that can be accomplished by skimming for facts. By establishing the questions you want answered before you begin to read, you can quickly browse through the material, only extracting the information you need.

Let's say you are reading a history text with the goal of identifying the key players in the Watergate Affair. You can dash through the section that paints a picture of the day's political scene. You can whiz through the description of the Watergate Towers. And you can briefly skim the highlights of other questionable and clandestine political activity in American history. You know what – or who – you are looking for. And there they are – Chuck Colson, John Dean, Mitchell, Liddy – the whole gang. Now you can start to *read*.

By identifying the questions you wanted to answer (*aka* your purpose) in advance, you would be able to skim the chapter and answer your questions in a lot less time than it would have taken painstakingly to read every word.

As a general rule, if you are reading textbook material word for word, you are probably wasting quite a bit of your study time. Good readers are able to discern what they should read in this manner and what they can afford to skim. When trying simply to gather detail and facts, skimming a text is a simple and very important shortcut.

Alternatively, your ability to skim a chapter – even something you need to read more critically – will enable you to develop a general sense of what the chapter is about and how thoroughly it needs to be read.

**Exercise**: Answer the following questions by skimming the paragraph that follows.

1  How many days are there in an astronomical year?

2  Calendar years have how many days? Hours? Minutes? Seconds?

3  To regain the fraction of a day lost each calendar year, what is done?

Why do we have leap years? They occur to make up the day lost by the fact that our calendar year and the astronomical year do not coincide exactly. An astronomical year has 2,424 days. In calendar years, this is 365 days, five hours, 45 minutes, and 12 seconds. The extra fraction of a day is made up by what we call leap years – when we add an extra day to February. This is done to keep our calendar year in step with the seasons, which are based on the astronomical year.

If this were part of your assigned reading, you would have completed it when you had answered the questions. "But I didn't read it", you protest. Can you write a one-sentence summary of the paragraph? If you can, and you answered the questions correctly, then you know all you need to.

Skimming, or prereading, is a valuable step even if you are not seeking specific facts. When skimming for a general overview, there is a very simple procedure to follow.

1 If there is a title or heading, *rephrase it as a question*. This will be your purpose for reading.

2 Examine all the *subheadings, illustrations and graphics*, as these will help you identify the significant matter within the text.

3 Read thoroughly the *introductory paragraphs*, the summary and any questions at the end of the chapter.

4 Read the *first sentence* of every paragraph. As we found in Chapter 3, this is generally where the main idea of a text is found.

5 *Evaluate* what you have gained from this process. Can you answer the questions at the end of the chapter? Could you intelligently participate in a classroom discussion of the material?

6 *Write* a brief summary that encapsulates what you have learned from your skimming.

7 Based on this evaluation, *decide* whether a more thorough reading is required.

**Exercise**: See how well you can skim for an overview, rather than for specific facts. Read the following two passages, then follow the seven steps outlined above for each one.

Five major scandals tainted the administration of President Ulysses S Grant. Although the hero of Vicksburg was the first president to encounter charges of substantial wrongdoing during his administration, it was never proved that he was directly involved in any criminal acts nor that he profited from any of the acts of others.

The first incident occurred in 1869, the first year of his presidency. Known as Black Friday, it involved speculators James Fisk and Jay Gould and their attempt to corner the gold market. By involving Grant's brother-in-law, they hoped to prevent the government from 'dumping' its gold on to the market, which would make it impossible for their scheme to succeed. Grant was not directly involved in Fisk's and Gould's machinations, but he certainly gave the appearance of complicity, allowing himself to be entertained lavishly and publicly on Fisk's yacht. However, when the pair's aggressive purchases of gold sent its price skyrocketing in a matter of days, Grant acted swiftly, ordering the Treasury Department to sell off $4 million in gold reserves. While this ended Fisk's and Gould's attempt, this step brought ruin to a number of individuals and businesses that were 'riding the wave' of gold fever and resulted in a national economic shock not matched until the 1929 stock market crash.

The second major scandal involved the embezzlement of massive amounts of money by the Credit Mobilier holding company, which was involved with the construction of the Union Pacific railway. To avoid being discovered, the conspirators heavily bribed members of Congress and officials of the Republican Party, of which Grant was the nominal head. Although this scandal erupted during a heated re-election campaign against newspaper publisher Horace Greeley, Grant was evidently completely uninvolved and was re-elected.

Two other scandals involved taxes and the officials appointed to collect them. One tax collector, John Sanborn, managed to keep nearly half of the delinquent taxes he collected, a total that exceeded $200,000. But that paled in comparison to the fraud discovered by Treasury Secretary Benjamin H Bristow among liquor distillers and the officials charged with collecting taxes from them. Although Grant called for swift action against all the conspirators, his fervour flagged when his trusted personal secretary, Orville Babcock, was implicated in the scheme. Although Grant slowed the investigation, 110 conspirators were eventually found guilty.

In the final year of Grant's second term, evidence mounted that Secretary of War W W Belknap had been taking bribes from corrupt white traders at Indian trading posts. Since Grant had made much of his earlier attempts to institute a fair and non-abusive set of policies towards the Indians, the scandal was a personal embarrassment, though, again, Grant was in no way directly involved. Faced with certain impeachment, Belknap resigned.

◆ ▮ ◆ ▮ ◆ ▮ ◆

### Self-fulfilling prophecies and other scientific marvels*

A combination of proper analytic skills and common sense is required for an executive to be effective. Call it the place where art and science meet. When you have the overly scientific, you find yourself in Dr Frankenstein's laboratory, which I did one day at a large consumer products company in California.

The organisation was looking at a decline in business caused by a combination of more aggressive competition and their own failure to launch some new products that their plan had heavily relied on. So the employees were going to bear the brunt of management's failure in these two areas. A senior management meeting was held to decide how best to downsize and to create several levels of contingency to react to various levels of revenue losses (and various degrees of shareholder ire). You see, it is simple to earn big bucks; the management team was putting a hierarchy of firings in place to deal with a bad year, a horrible year and a disastrous year. Imagine what would have happened if this talent and time had been devoted to trying to *improve* the year.

---

*Adapted from *Our Emperors Have No Clothes* by Alan Weiss (Career Press, 1995)

A particularly officious young woman from staffing and planning was invited to the meeting to provide some of the details of implementing the phased reductions. As the session progressed, I became mesmerised by her high-tech language for what was, to me, a highly emotive problem. When asked at what point the second level of discharges would begin, for example, she replied:

'Attrits from the prime round should have been in the outplace mode, offsite, if they were of grades 8 or higher. Other attrits would simply be gone. If profit levels for the second quarter fall below 85 per cent of plan as determined by this group, I will initiate secondary attrits. Human resources will inform and escort on the same day, which we advise be a Friday, if possible. Tertiary attrits will occur if profit falls below 75 per cent of plan. Tertiary attrits will receive no outplace assistance, unless they are supergrade.'

What this all meant, I deciphered, was that the people being let go were being referred to as 'attrits' (short for attrition). This helped dehumanise the situation significantly. We could have been discussing reducing inventory or equipment leases.

This was a case of all head, all science. It was a pragmatic approach using computer-like precision to remove people as though they were merely expense items on a balance sheet. The result was disastrous for morale and did not address the underlying cause of the company's market-place problems.

---

While it may not be evident at first, you will soon see how skimming can save you a lot of reading time. Even if a more in-depth reading is necessary, you will find that having gone through this process, you will have developed the kind of skeletal framework that will make your further reading faster, easier and more meaningful. If all you need is 'just the facts, ma'am', your ability to scan a passage, chapter or book will save you minutes, if not hours, every week.

Whether you are skimming or scanning, you will have equipped yourself with the ability to digest better what it is the author is trying to communicate.

# 5 The challenge of technical writing

You have already learned many ways to improve your reading. It is time to examine the unique challenges posed by highly technical writing. Physics, trigonometry, chemistry, calculus – you know, the subjects that three-quarters of all students try to avoid, unless they have a particular affinity with or need for them.

Compared to any other kind of reading, these subjects demand a logical, organised approach, a step-by-step reading method.

They also require a detection of the text's organisational devices.

Developing the skill to identify the basic sequence of the text will enable you to follow the progression of thought, a progression that is vital to your comprehension and retention.

Why? In most technical writing, each concept is like a building block of understanding – if you do not understand a particular section or concept, you will not be able to understand the next section, either.

Most technical books are saturated with ideas, terms, formulas and theories. The chapters are dense with information, compressing a wealth of ideas into a small space. They demand to be read very carefully.

In order to get as much as possible from such reading assignments, you can take advantage of some devices to make sense of the organisation. Here are five basics to look out for:

1 Definitions and terms.

2 Examples.

3 Classifications and listings.

4 Use of contrast.

5 Cause–effect relationships.

As you read any text, but certainly a highly specialised one, identifying these devices will help you grasp the main idea, as well as any details that are essential to your thorough understanding of the material.

## Definitions and terminology

In reading any specialised text, you must begin at the beginning – understanding the terms particular to that discipline. Familiar, everyday words have very precise definitions in technical writing.

What do I mean? Take the word *nice*. You may compliment your friend's new sweater, telling her it is *nice*, meaning attractive. You may find that the new chemistry teacher is *nice*, meaning he does not give too much homework. And when your friend uses the word *nice* to describe the blind date she has set up for you, it may mean something completely different – and insidious.

Everyday words can have a variety of meanings, some of them even contradictory, depending on the context in which they are used.

In contrast, in the sciences, terminology has fixed and specific meanings . For example, the definition of elasticity – 'the ability of a solid to regain its shape after a deforming force has been applied' is the same in Bangkok or Birmingham. Such exact terminology enables scientists to communicate with the precision their discipline requires.

Definitions may vary in length. One term may require a one-sentence definition, others merit entire paragraphs. Some may need a whole chapter to accurately communicate the definition.

## Examples help clarify the abstract

A second communication tool is the example. Authors use examples to bridge abstract principles to concrete illustrations. These examples are essential to your ability to comprehend intricate and complicated theories.

Unlike other writing, technical writing places a very high premium on brevity. Economising on words is the key to covering a large volume of knowledge in a relatively small space. Few technical texts or articles include anecdotal matter or chatty stories of the author's experience.

This fact challenges the reader to pay particular attention to the examples that are included. Why? Technical writing is often filled with new or foreign ideas – many of which are not readily digestible. They are difficult in part because they are abstract. Examples work to clarify these concepts, hopefully in terms more easily understood. For example, it may be difficult for you to make sense of the definition of symbiosis – 'the living together of two dissimilar organisms, especially when mutually beneficial' – but the example of the bird that picks food from the crocodile's teeth, at the same time feeding itself and keeping the crocodile cavity free, helps bring it home.

## Classification and listings

A third tool frequently utilised in texts is classification and listings. Classifying is the process by which common subjects are categorised under a general heading.
Some examples:

*Matter may occur in three forms: solid, liquid or gas.*
**Classification**: Three forms of matter
**Listing**: Solid, liquid, gas

*The social sciences are psychology, economics and sociology.*
**Classification**: Social sciences
**Listing**: Psychology, economics, sociology

Particularly in technical writing, authors use classification to categorise extensive lists of detail. Such writings may have several categories and subcategories that organise these details into some manageable fashion.

## Comparing/contrasting

A fourth tool used in communicating difficult information is that of comparing and contrasting. Texts use this tool to bring complicated material into focus by offering a similar or opposing picture.
Such devices are invaluable in grasping concepts that do not conjure a picture in your mind. Gravity, for example, is not something that can be readily pictured – it is not a tangible object that can be described.

Through comparison, a text relates a concept to one that has been previously defined – or to one a reader may readily understand. Through contrast, the text concentrates on the differences and distinctions between two ideas. By focusing on distinguishing features, these ideas become clearer as one idea is held up against another.

## Cause–effect relationships

A final tool that texts employ to communicate is the cause–effect relationship. This device is best defined in the context of science, where it is the fundamental quest of most scientific research.

Science begins with the observation of the effect – what is happening?

It is snowing.

The next step is to conduct research into the cause. Why is it snowing? Detailing this cause–effect relationship is often the essence of scientific and technical writing.

Cause–effect relationships can be written in many ways. The effect may be stated first, followed by the cause. An effect may be the result of several connected causes – a causal chain. And a cause may have numerous effects.

In your reading, it is vital that you recognise this relationship and its significance.

## Read with a plan

More than any other type of writing, highly specialised, technical writing must be read with a plan. You cannot approach your reading assignment merely with the goal of completing it. Such mindless reading will leave you confused and frustrated, drowning in a sea of theory, concepts, terms and examples.

Your plan should incorporate the following guidelines.

1 **Learn the terms** that are essential to understand the concepts presented. Knowing the precise definitions that the author uses will enable you to follow his chain of thought throughout the text.

2 **Determine the structure or organisation of the text**. Most chapters have a definite pattern that forms the skeleton of the material. A book may begin with a statement of a theory, give examples, provide sample problems, then summarise. Often this pattern can be discerned through a preview of the table of contents or the titles and subtitles.

3 **Skim the chapter** to get a sense of the author's viewpoint. Ask questions to define your purpose in reading. Use any summaries or review questions to guide your reading.

4 **Do a thorough analytical reading of the text**. Do not proceed from one section to the next until you have a clear understanding of the section you are reading – the concepts generally build upon each other. To proceed to a new section without understanding the ones that precede it is, at best, futile.

5 **Immediately upon concluding your thorough reading, review**. Write a summary of the concepts and theories you need to remember. Answer any questions raised when you skimmed the text. Do the problems. If possible, apply the formulas.

Technical material is saturated with ideas. When reading it, you must be convinced of one fact: every individual word counts. You will want to read such material with the utmost concentration – it is not meant to be sped through.

Good readers know that such material demands a slow read that concentrates on achieving the greatest level of retention.

▌ Every definition has to be digested.

▌ Every formula must be committed to memory.

▌ Every example needs to be considered.

To improve your reading of such technical material you will want to improve on the skill of identifying the devices an author uses to communicate. In so doing, you will be able to connect the chain of thought that occurs. When reading such texts – or attempting to work out technical problems – try the following 'tricks'.

▮ Whenever you can, 'translate' formulas and numbers into words. To test your understanding, try to put your translation into different words.

▮ Even if you are not particularly visual, pictures can often help. You should try translating a particularly difficult maths problem into a drawing or diagram.

▮ Before you begin to solve a problem, is there any way you can estimate the answer or, at least, estimate the range within which the answer should fall (greater than one, but less than 10)? This is the easy way to make sure you end up in the right area.

▮ Play around. There are often different paths to the same solution, or even equally valid solutions. If you find one, try to find others. This is a great way to increase your understanding of all the principles involved.

▮ When you are checking your calculations, try working backwards. I have found it an easier way to catch simple mathematical errors.

▮ Try to work out what is being asked, what principles are involved, what information is important and what is not.

▮ Teach someone else. Trying to explain mathematical concepts to someone else will quickly pinpoint what you really know or do not know. It is virtually impossible to get someone else – especially someone who is slower than you in this subject – to understand if you don't.

# 6 Becoming a critical reader

After four years of undergraduate work, before my old university would award me my degree, I was made to endure a six-hour essay exam. We were given one question in this literature exam – 'Analyse and interpret the following' (the 'following' being a poem we had never seen before... and a large amount of paper on which to write our erudite answers).

Unbelievable?

Hardly!

This exam was set in much the same way that many GCSE and A level exams are. In the reading comprehension section, you are expected to read a passage you have never seen – and then given four to six questions to answer, to determine if you have any clue as to what you just read.

You will find that there are many times, particularly in comparative literature classes, when you will need to read something with great care in order to remember details and interpret meaning. Many of the passages will require a little more analysis than a superficial interpretation of props and plot.

Yet such detailed, analytical reading is not limited to literature. Political dissertations, historical analysis and even scientific research may require more careful reading than the latest 'soap opera'.

This reading is often referred to as *critical reading*, a type of reading where you try to distinguish thoughts, ideas or concepts – each demanding thorough study and evaluation.

Critical reading requires you to identify the author's arguments, measure their worth and truth and apply what is pertinent to your own experience. Unlike skimming, critical reading challenges the reader to concentrate at the highest level possible.

## Prepare yourself to read critically

When preparing to read critically, you must lay the ground-work for concentration. Just as an athlete must ready himself mentally to achieve peak performance, you will want to prepare yourself before you begin to read.

Keep the following in mind as you prepare to read critically.

1   You must have a clearly defined purpose for reading. Make sure that you have identified your purpose before you begin.

2   Pay attention! Avoid letting your mind wander to that conversation you and your friend had today at lunchtime. Minimise distractions and interruptions – anything or anyone that causes you to break your focus.

3   Find your optimum study environment – a quiet corner in the library, your own room, etc. In absolute silence, or with your new CD playing. (More tips on finding your perfect study environment are discussed in two other books in this series.)

4   Do not concern yourself with how fast or slowly you read. Your goal should be to understand the material, not to find out how fast you can get it over with.

5   If it seems that you will need several hours to complete your reading, you could break the longer assignments into smaller, more manageable parts, then reward yourself at the end of each of these sections by taking short breaks.

If you take these steps prior to reading any text that needs your utmost concentration, you will find that your mind is prepared for the kind of focus necessary to read critically. Make a habit of such preparations and you will be well set up to succeed.

## Prereading is a must

Once you have prepared your mind to read, the next step is to understand the big picture – what is the author's thesis or main idea? Good comprehension is the consequence of your ability to grasp the main point of what the author is trying to communicate.

Grasping this message is accomplished through skimming the text, as we discussed in Chapter 4. Let's review the basic steps.

1 If there is a title or heading, rephrase it as a question. This will support your purpose for reading.

2 Examine all subheadings, illustrations and graphics, as these will help you identify the significant matter within the text.

3 Read the introductory paragraphs, summary and any questions at the end of the chapter.

4 Read the first sentence of every paragraph. In Chapter 3 you learned that this is generally where the main idea is found.

5 Evaluate what you have gained from this process. Can you answer the questions at the end of the chapter? Could you intelligently participate in a classroom discussion of the material?

6 Write a brief summary of what you have learned from your skimming.

By beginning critical reading with a 20-minute skim of the text, you should be ready to answer these three questions.

1 What is the text's principal message, or viewpoint?

2 Is an obvious chain of thought or reasoning revealed?

3 What major points are addressed?

## Now, read it

Once you identify and understand the basic skeleton of the material, your actual 'read' of the material – following the details, reasoning and chain of thought – is simply a matter of attaching the body to the bones.

This digestive process involves learning to interpret and evaluate what is written, what is directly stated and what can be inferred from the context.

Effective analytical reading necessitates that you, the reader, distinguish the explicit, literal meaning of words (denotation) and what suggestions or intentions are intimated by the general content (connotation).

## Analysing: what the words connote (imply)

Words and writing have two levels of meaning that are important to the reader's comprehension.

The first level is the literal or descriptive meaning. What a word expressly denotes means the specific, precise definition you would find in your dictionary.

Connotation involves the second level of meaning – that which incorporates the total significance of the words.

What does that mean? Beyond a literal definition, words communicate emotion, bias, attitude and perspective. Analysing any text involves learning to interpret what is implied, just as much as what is expressly stated.

### *Questions to help you*

Beyond grasping the meaning of words and phrases, critical reading insists that you ask questions. Here are 15 questions that will help you effectively analyse and interpret most of what you read.

1 Is there a clear message communicated throughout?

2 Are the relationships between the points direct and clear?

3 Is there a relationship between your experience and the author's?

4  Are the details factual?

5  Are the examples and evidence relevant?

6  Is there consistency of thought?

7  What is the author's bias or slant?

8  What is the author's motive?

9  What does the author want you to believe?

10  Does this agree with your own beliefs or experiences?

11  Is the author rational or subjective?

12  Is there a confusion between feelings and facts?

13  Are the main points logically ordered?

14  Are the arguments and conclusions consistent?

15  Are the explanations clear?

Obviously, this list of questions is not all-inclusive, but it will give you a jump-start when critical reading is needed. Remember, the essential ingredient of any effective analysis and interpretation is the questions you ask.

## Summarising: the final step

Nothing will be more important to your recall than learning to condense what you read into a clear and concise summary.

Many of you have learned to do this by excerpting entire segments or sentences from a text, which is certainly not a very efficient method for summarising.

One suggestion is to use a two-step process called *diagramming*, which asks the reader to diagram or illustrate the content he has just read, then write a brief synopsis of what he has learned.

Similar to outlining, diagramming helps the reader to visualise the relationships between various thoughts and ideas. Concept diagrams, or concept trees, are very useful visual aids for depicting the structure of a textbook.

Unless you have a photographic memory, you will find that recognising a picture of the main points will greatly increase what you remember. These diagrams also require you to distil what is essential to the text and how it relates to the main message.

Suppose you read a chapter in your biology assignment about the parts of a cell. Your diagram might reduce your reading material to look like the following.

---

**Parts of a Cell**

| Outside of Cell | Inside of Cell |
|---|---|
| cell wall | cytoplasm |
| cell membrane | vacuoles |
| nucleus chloroplasts | chlorophyll |

---

More than a listing of main points, a diagram allows you to picture how parts fit together, which enhances your ability to recall the information you have read. This is especially true the more 'visual' you are.

## Distil it into a synopsis

The second step in the process of summarising is to write a brief synopsis of what you have learned. When you need to review the material, diagrams will remind you of the significant elements in the text. Your synopsis will remind you of the main idea.

The goal here is to put into your own words what you gleaned from what you read. You will find this process an invaluable gauge of whether you have understood the message – and on what level.

Use this method one chapter at a time and do not proceed to the next chapter until you have completed the following exercise.

1 Write definitions of any key terms you feel are essential for understanding the topic.

2 Write questions and answers you feel clarify the topic.

3 Write any questions for which you do not have answers – then make sure you find them through rereading, further research or asking another student or your teacher.

4 If you still have unanswered questions, move on to the next section and complete numbers one to three for that section. (And so on, until your reading assignment is complete.)

See if this method helps you get a better handle on any assignment right from the start.

Critical reading is not easy. It requires a lot more concentration and effort than the quick-reference reading that you can get away with for much of your day-to-day classroom assignments. Much of the reading you will do in the latter years of secondary school and throughout college and university will be critical reading.

However, if you follow the steps I have outlined for each critical reading assignment that you tackle – preparing yourself for the read, doing a preread skim, followed by an analytical reading, concluding with a summation – you will discover that critical reading can be a much smoother, even rewarding, experience.

## The method you probably learned

If you were taught a specific reading method at school, it was probably the one developed back in the 1940s that is abbreviated to 'SQ3R'. This stands for Survey, Question, Read, Recite and Review. This is how the process works.

▌ **Survey**. Preread the chapter, concentrating on topic sentences, subheads and review questions, so as to get an overview of what is ahead.

▌ **Question**. Once you have surveyed the chapter, ask yourself what information is contained in it. Consider turning the subheads into questions as an exercise.

▌ **Read**. Now read the first section thoroughly, attempting to answer the questions you have posed. Take notes, highlight, underline, map.

▌ **Recite**. Now answer the questions without looking at your notes or the text. When you have completed this, go on to the next section. Continue this detailed reading/reciting tandem until you complete the chapter (or the assignment).

▌ **Review**. Go back over the entire assignment.

Does this sound familiar? I agree. I think this method is completely incorporated in the steps I have outlined in this and previous chapters. I think the detailed method I have proposed – and the helpful advice along the way – also covers far more ground.

# 7 *Reading literature*

"Will you walk a little faster?" said a whiting to a snail.
"There's a porpoise close behind us and he's treading on my tail!"

"If I'd been the whiting," said Alice, whose thoughts were still running on the song, "I'd have said to the porpoise, "'Keep back, please; we don't want you with us!'"

"They were obliged to have him with them," the Mock Turtle said. "No wise fish would go anywhere without a porpoise."

"Wouldn't it really?" said Alice in a tone of great surprise.

"Of course not," said the Mock Turtle. "Why, if a fish came to me, and told me he was going on a journey, I should say, 'With what porpoise?'"

"Don't you mean purpose?" said Alice.

"I mean what I say," the Mock Turtle replied in an offended tone.

LEWIS CARROLL, *Alice in Wonderland*

In this excerpt, you could enjoy the nonsensical picture of a porpoise pushing a snail and whiting to walk faster. You might laugh at the confusion of 'porpoise' and 'purpose' by the Mock Turtle. Or you could discern the message – that you need to have a purpose when you are on a journey... or reading.

In today's world of Sega, Mortal Kombat and and all the other computer games, literature often takes a back seat. So much so that many of your classmates (not you, of course) may not even know that *Alice in Wonderland* is an important piece of literature.

Why should you care about literature? Who needs to read the book when you can see the film? While I did not write this book to give you a lecture on the merits of the classics, please bear with me for a couple of paragraphs.

## The greatest involvement device

Unlike anything else, literature involves the reader in the story. How? There are no joysticks to manipulate, no surround-a-sound to engulf you. Your imagination is your only involvement device, but it far surpasses any high-tech computer gimmicks.

Your imagination makes reading the ultimate adventure. It allows you to immerse yourself in the story – identifying with the protagonist, fighting his battles, experiencing his fears, sharing his victories. You may become so involved, you end up staying up most of the night, turning page after page!

Your imagination is the vehicle that allows you to explore a million different lives, from floating down the Mississippi River on a raft, to suffering through a star-crossed love affair, to having tea with the March Hare and the Mad Hatter, as Alice did.

Creative writing may be serious or humorous or sublime… or all three. It is often subtle; meanings are elusive and delicate. Such writing, when done effectively, evokes emotional responses. You get angry. You shed a tear. You chuckle. An author's expression strikes a chord that moves you. You and the author communicate on a level that is far beyond an exchange of facts and information.

Enough said. Assuming that I have converted all you literature skeptics to avid library loiterers (and even if I have not), I will offer some advice to help you begin your journey to literary appreciation. It begins with understanding the basic road-map.

## Which reading method? Pleasure or critical?

While I certainly encourage you to approach your reading with the enthusiasm and anticipation that would justify the pleasure-reading method (see Chapter 2), the demands of your teacher who assigns the reading will probably require the *critical* reading method.

Reading literature requires most of the skills we have discussed previously.

There are devices and clues to search for that will help you follow the story and understand its meaning better.

You will analyse and interpret what the author is saying and evaluate its worth.

But in addition, in literature, you will be able to appreciate the words themselves. In textbooks, you must often penetrate a thick jungle of tangled sentences and murky paragraphs to find the information you seek.

Great literature is its language. It is the flow and ebb of its words, the cadence of its sentences, as much as it is story and theme.

As you read more, you will uncover the diversity of tapestries that different authors weave with words. You may discover similar themes coursing through the works of authors like Ernest Hemingway or Thomas Hardy, but their use of language is as different as desert and forest. The composition of the words themselves is an element you will want to examine as you critically read literature.

## Fiction: just another word for story-telling

Most fiction is an attempt to tell a story. There is a *beginning*, in which the characters and the setting are introduced. There is a *conflict* or *struggle* (middle) that advances the story to a *climax* (end) – where the conflict is resolved. A final denouement or 'winding up' clarifies the conclusion of the story.

Your literature class will address all of these parts using literary terms that are often more confusing than helpful. The following are brief descriptions of some of the more important ones.

▌ **Plot**. The order or sequence of the story – how it proceeds from the opening through the climax. Your ability to understand and appreciate literature depends upon how well you follow the plot – the story.

▌ **Characterisation**. The personalities or characters central to the story – the heroes, heroines and villains. You will want to identify the main characters of the story and their relationship to the struggle or conflict. Pay particular attention as to whether the characters are three dimensional – are they real and believable?

▪ **Theme**. The controlling message or subject of the story; the moral or idea that the author is using the plot and characters to communicate. Some examples: man's inhumanity to man, man's impotency in his environment, the corrupting influence of power, greed and unrequited love. Just as with nonfiction, you need to discern this theme to really understand what it is the author wants to communicate.

▪ **Setting**. The time and place in which the story takes place. This is especially important when reading a historical novel or one that takes you to another culture.

▪ **Point of view**. Who is telling the story? Is it one of the central characters giving you flashbacks or a first-person perspective? Or is it a third-person narrator offering commentary and observations on the characters, the setting and the plot? This person moves the story along and gives it an overall tone.

The first step in reading literature is to familiarise yourself with these concepts and then to try to recognise them in each novel or short story you read.

The second step is the same as for reading nonfiction – to identify your purpose for reading.

Allow your purpose to define how you will read. If you are reading to be entertained, then a pleasure read is the way to go. If you are reading for a course and will be expected to participate in discussions or be tested on the material, you will want to do a critical read.

## How long should it take?

As a general rule, fiction is not meant to be read over a period of months – or even weeks. Try to read it as quickly as possible to get a full appreciation of the author's plot, character and theme. You should read fast enough to progress through the plot, get a sense of the characters and their struggles and hear the author's message or theme.

It is helpful to set a goal for when you want to complete your reading. Frequently, of course, this will already be set for you, if your reading is a classroom assignment.

You should, however, set daily goals. Set aside one or two hours to read, or set a goal of reading three chapters a day until you have read the whole book. Reading sporadically – ten minutes one day, a half-hour the next, then not picking up the book until several days later – means that you will lose track of the plot and characters and just as quickly lose interest.

Too often when students do not establish a regular schedule, their reading becomes fragmented, making it very difficult to piece together the whole story. A reasonable goal is to try to read a novel in less than a week, a short story in one sitting. To achieve this goal, once you begin, you should read every day until you have finished it. By doing this, the story and characters will stay fresh in your mind.

If you try to read fiction more rapidly, you will greatly increase your enjoyment of it. It is vitally important that as you try to read faster, you give the story your full attention. By doing this you will be surprised by how improved your understanding and appreciation are.

To speed up your reading of fiction, try this experiment.

1  Find a novel or short story that interests you and is relatively easy to read. Tomes like *Ulysses* or *War and Peace* should not be candidates.

2  Set aside two or three hours to invest in reading the book. If at all possible, complete it in one sitting. If you cannot, then allocate the same amount of time each day until you do.

By trying this experiment, you will discover that fiction is intended to be read this way – whenever possible, in one sitting. It is as if you are sitting at a master story-teller's feet as he spins his tale. You want to know how the story ends and what happens to the hero.

Will the villain get his comeuppance? Will the hero get the girl? Or ride off with his horse?

You will find that you appreciate the story far more at the end than anywhere in the middle.

Some other tips for reading fiction:

1 Understand the plot and maintain awareness of its progression.

2 Take breaks to review what has occurred and who is involved.

3 Vary your reading method – from skimming transitional bridge material to carefully reading description and narration.

4 Question the story's theme. What is the message?

## You are allowed to enjoy it

A final recommendation. Give yourself permission to enjoy what you are reading. You will be amazed at the difference this will make. Fiction, unlike any other reading, can take you on an adventure. Through your mind, you can journey to faraway lands, pretend you are someone else, feel emotions you may never otherwise experience. All this happens as you gain an appreciation of literature – as you learn to understand fiction and allow yourself to enjoy great stories.

**Focusing your mind**

Concentration is one of the biggest challenges facing any reader.

Why? Unlike other activities, reading requires an active mind and a passive body. A deadly combination, especially when you have spent the day in the classroom or at lectures and have not had a chance to burn off that excess energy with a tennis match, a game of football or a quick jog.

As regards concentration, reading can be more demanding than classroom lectures, homework assignments or note-taking. In the classroom, you at least have vocal variety and the threat of being called upon to keep you focused. And writing, while a sedentary activity, still requires some hand–eye coordination to keep your brain working.

## Keep your mind on one thing

Concentration begins with the ability to keep your mind focused on one thing – your reading assignment. This is not an innate talent, but a learned discipline. Much like an athlete must learn to be so focused that she is completely unaffected by the screaming crowds, a good reader absorbs himself in what he is reading.

How does *your* 'mind discipline' rate? Answer these questions to find out.

1 When I read, do I often allow random thoughts to steal my focus?

2 As I read, am I easily distracted by noises or other activities?

3 Am I watching the clock to see how long I have been reading?

There is no simple, magic formula for conjuring up concentration – especially when you are faced with a critical reading assignment you are not particularly looking forward to. But if you follow the preparatory steps I have discussed in previous chapters – define your purpose, skim for a preread, identify questions for which you will seek answers – you should find it a bit easier to stay focused.

## Steps to better concentration

Here are some other practical steps I recommend to increase your ability to concentrate.

1  **Do some exercise** before you begin your reading. A game of football, an exercise class, a workout at the gym, even a brisk walk, will help burn off physical energy so you will be able to direct all of your mental energy to your reading.

2  **Read in the right place.** No, it is not in front of the TV, nor in your room if your roommate is throwing a pizza party. Reading is a solitary activity. Find a quiet corner, preferably in a place designated for study only – at your desk, in the library. Although tempting, reading on your bed can be dangerous if you are struggling to concentrate. You just may lose the battle and find yourself in the perfect place to doze off.

3  **Eliminate distractions**. If you have properly scheduled your reading time, you will not be distracted by other pending assignments. If you are trying to read one assignment while worrying about another, your concentration – and comprehension – will inevitably suffer.

   Make sure there is nothing else in sight to vie for your attention. Are there letters on your desk that you need to respond to? Put them away and schedule some time to write them. Sirens and screams from the TV programme in the other room? Turn it off, lower the volume or close your door.

4 **Plan breaks**. If you have three hours or more of reading ahead of you, the mere thought of it may be so discouraging that you will lose your concentration before you even pick up the book. Schedule short 10- or 15-minute breaks after each hour of reading. Get up. Listen to some music. Stretch. If you must break more frequently, keep your breaks shorter. By breaking up your reading into smaller, more digestible bites, you will be able to concentrate more effectively.

Wait! Don't start reading yet.

Have you defined your purpose for reading? Once again, you must have a clearly defined purpose or goal. What are you reading for? (We have addressed this numerous times, but spaced repetition is a very effective way to make a point.)

The point is that reading without purpose is the greatest means to getting nowhere, which is where you will find your mind after about half an hour.

Know why you are reading. If your teacher or tutor has given you questions to answer, then you know what you are looking for. If not, ask your own questions, using the clues in your book (as discussed in Chapter 2).

An effective preread of the material should help you define your purpose and stimulate some interest in finding out more – which will result in increased concentration.

## Motivation: crucial to concentration

Motivation is key to your success in almost any endeavour, whether it is graduating with honours at university, maintaining an effective time management programme or improving your reading. You can utilise all the tricks and steps I have mentioned in this chapter, but if you lack the motivation to read, you will still find it a struggle to concentrate on your assignments.

There are two types of motivation – intrinsic and extrinsic. What is the difference?

As an avid murder mystery fan, you buy stacks of paperbacks at the secondhand bookshop and spend your free time with your nose buried in them. You love the challenge of working out 'who did it' before you reach the end. In fact, you could spend all weekend reading mysteries if you did not have to complete a reading assignment for your political science class. You are not particularly interested in political science, but your efforts on this assignment could secure you an A for the term, so you are determined to read the material and sail through the exam

Your motivation for reading the mysteries is intrinsic – you do it because you enjoy it. You do not get any awards. You do not get paid for it.

The political science reading, on the other hand, requires external motivation. You are reading it because you want to earn a high mark for your assignment. Your reward is external – beyond the reading itself.

Whether you are intrinsically motivated to read or doing it for some external reward does not matter as much as the fact that you are motivated by something. If you find it difficult to get excited about reading your economics assignment, remind yourself of how this exercise will help your mark – get yourself externally motivated.

If that does not get you motivated enough to read for three hours, there is nothing wrong with a little bribery. Reward yourself with something more immediate. Promise yourself that if you stay focused on your reading until it is completed, you can watch that video afterwards. Or you can buy that new CD. (Be careful, though. If you need lots of extrinsic motivation, you could run out of money!)

The value of concentration can be summed up in one statement. Concentration is essential to comprehension. Where there is failure to focus, there will be little or no understanding.

Without concentration, you will see only words on a page.

# 9 Retaining the information

The ultimate test of your comprehension is what you remember after you have completed your reading – what you walk away with.

As a student, most of your reading will be for courses in which, sooner or later, you will be required to regurgitate the information you have read in some type of format – essay, test, end of term exam, multiple-choice, true-false or fill-in-the-blank questions.

So, more than just being able to complete your reading assignments, you want to make sure you remember what you read.

All of you have probably had the experience of forgetting that important fact that made the difference between an A- and a B+ (or a B- and a C+). It was sitting right there, on the tip of your brain. But you could not quite remember it.

## Memory can be improved

You probably know people with photographic (or near-photographic) memories. They know all the words to all the songs in *Rolling Stone's* Top Fifty, remind you of things you said to them three years ago and never forget anyone's birthday (or anniversary or 'day we met' or 'first kiss day', *ad infinitum*).

While some people seem to be able to retain information naturally, a good memory – like good concentration – can be learned. You can control what stays in your mind and what is forgotten. The key to this control is to learn and tap into the essential elements of good memory.

Some people remember with relative ease and have no problem retaining large volumes of information. Others are often aggravated by a faulty memory that seems to lose more than it retains. Several factors contribute to your capability to recall the information you take in.

▌ **Intelligence, age and experience** all play a role in how well you remember. Not everyone remembers in the same way. You need to identify how these factors affect your memory and learn to maximise your strengths.

▌ **Laying a strong foundation** is important to good memory. Most learning is an addition to something you already know. If you never grasped basic chemistry, then mastering organic chemistry will be virtually impossible. By developing a broad base of basic knowledge, you will enhance your ability to recall new information.

▌ **Motivation is key** to improving your memory. A friend of mine, the consummate football fan, seems to know every football statistic from the beginning of time. He can spout off goals scored and team transfers from any decade for virtually any player, his favourite team's fixtures for the season... and most of the other teams', too. While I wouldn't say he is the most intelligent man I have ever met, he obviously loves football and is highly motivated to memorise as much as possible about his favourite subject.

You probably have a pet interest, too. Whether it is films, music or sports, you have filled your brain with a mountain of information. Now, if you can learn that much about one subject, you are obviously capable of retaining information about other subjects – even chemistry. You just have to learn how to motivate yourself.

▌ **A method, system or process** for retaining information is crucial to increasing your recall. This may include organising your thinking, good study habits or mnemonic devices – something you will use when you have to remember.

▌ **Using what you learn**, soon after you learn it, is important to recall. It is fine to memorise a vocabulary list for a quick test, but if you wish to retain information for the final exam, you must reinforce your learning by using this knowledge. For example, you will add a new word to your permanent vocabulary if you make a point of using it, correctly, in a conversation.

The study of foreign languages, for many, proves frustrating when there are no opportunities outside the classroom to practise speaking the language. That is why foreign-language students often join conversation groups or study abroad – to reinforce retention of what they have learned by using it.

## Why we forget

As you think about the elements of developing good memory, you can use them to address why you forget. The root of poor memory is usually found in one of the following areas.

1 We fail to make the material meaningful.

2 We did not learn prerequisite material.

3 We fail to grasp what is to be remembered.

4 We do not have the desire to remember.

5 We allow apathy or boredom to dictate how we learn.

6 We have no set habit for learning.

7 We are disorganised and inefficient in our use of study time.

8 We do not use the knowledge we have gained.

All of us are inundated with information every day, bombarded with facts, concepts and opinion. We are capable of absorbing some information simply because the media drench us with it. (I have never read *Hello*, nor do I intend to, but how could I not be aware of its reputation for featuring spreads of happy, smiling celebrity couples, who seem to split up on receipt of their fee?)

In order to retain most information, we have to make a concerted effort to do so. We must make this same effort with the material we read.

# How to remember

There are some basic tools that will help you remember what you read.

▎ **Understanding**. You will remember only what you understand. When you read something and grasp the message,
you have begun the process of retention. The way to test
this is to state the message in your own words. Can you
summarise the main idea? Unless you understand what is
being said, you will not be able to decide whether it is to be
remembered or discarded.

▎ **Desire**. Let me repeat: you remember what you *choose* to
remember. If you do not want to retain some piece of
information or do not believe you can, then you won't. To
remember the material, you must want to remember it and
be convinced that you will remember it.

▎ **Overlearn**. To insure that you retain material, you need to
go beyond simply doing the assignment. To really remember
what you learn, you should learn material thoroughly, or
overlearn. This involves prereading the text, doing a critical
read and having some definite means of review that
reinforces what you should have learned.

▎ **Systematise**. It is more difficult to remember random
thoughts or numbers than those organised in some pattern.
For example, which phone number is easier to remember:
538-6284 or 678-1234? Once you recognise the pattern in the
second number, it takes much less effort to remember than
the first. You should develop the ability to discern the
structure that exists and recall it when you try to remember.
Have a system to help you recall how information is
organised and connected.

▎ **Association**. It is helpful to attach or associate what you are
trying to recall to something you already have in your memory. Mentally link new material to existing knowledge so
that you are giving this new thought some context in your
mind.

If we take these principles and apply them to your reading assignment, we can develop a procedure that will increase what you remember from your reading.

## A procedure to improve recall
Each time you attempt to read something that you must recall, use this six-step process.

1 **Evaluate the material and define your purpose** for reading. Identify your interest level and get a sense of how difficult the material is.

2 **Choose appropriate reading techniques** for the purpose of your reading. If you are reading to grasp the main idea then that is what you will recall.

3 **Identify the important facts**. Remember what you need to. Identify associations that connect the details you must recall.

4 **Take notes**. Use your own words to give a synopsis of the main ideas. Use an outline, diagram or concept tree to show relationship and pattern. Your notes provide an important backup to your memory. Writing down key points will reinforce further your ability to remember.

5 **Review**. Test yourself on those things you must remember. Develop some system by which you review notes at least three times before you have to recall. The first review should be shortly after you have completed your reading, the second should come a few days later and the final should take place just before you are expected to recall. This process will help you avoid cramming sessions.

6 **Implement**. Find opportunities to use the knowledge you have gained. Study groups and classroom discussions are invaluable opportunities to implement what you have learned.

## Memorising and mnemonics

Up until now, we have concentrated on the fundamentals of remembering and retention. There are some specific methods to help you recall when you must remember a lot of specific facts. The first of these is memorisation – the process of trying to recall information word for word.

Memorise only when you are required to remember something for a relatively short time – when you have a history test on battle dates, a chemistry test on specific formulas or a vocabulary test in French.

When memorisation is required, you should do whatever is necessary to impress the exact information on your mind. Repetition is probably the most effective method. Write down the information on a 3 x 5 inch card and use it as a flash card. You must test yourself frequently to ensure that you know the information perfectly.

A second technique for recalling lots of details is mnemonics. A mnemonic device is used to help recall large bits of information which may or may not be logically connected. Such mnemonics are invaluable when you must remember facts not arranged in a clear fashion, items that are quite complicated and numerous items that are a part of a series.

One of the simplest methods is to try to remember just the first letter of a sequence. That is how **R**oy **G** **B**iv or **R**ichard **O**f **Y**ork **G**ave **B**attle **I**n **V**ain (the colours of the spectrum, in order from left to right – red, orange, yellow, green, blue, indigo, violet) came about. Or **E**very **G**ood **B**oy **D**eserves **F**avour, to remember the notes on the musical staff. Or, perhaps the simplest of all, **FACE**, to remember the notes in between. (The last three work opposite to Roy – using words to remember letters.) Of course, not many sequences work out so easily. If you tried to memorise the signs of the zodiac with this method, you would wind up with **A**ries, **T**aurus, **G**emini, **C**ancer, **L**eo, **V**irgo, **L**ibra, **S**corpio, **S**agittarius, **C**apricorn, **A**quarius, **P**isces. Now many of you may be able to make a name, a place or something out of ATGCLVLSSCAP, but I can't.

One solution is to make up a simple sentence that uses the first letters of the list you are trying to remember as the first letters of each word. For example, **A** **T**all **G**iraffe **C**hewed **L**eaves **V**ery **L**ow, **S**ome **S**low **C**ows **A**t **P**lay.

Wait a minute! That's the same number of words. Why not just work out some way to memorise the first set of words? What is better about the second set? Two things. First of all, it is easier to picture the giraffe and cow and what they are doing. Creating mental images is a very powerful way to remember almost anything. Second, because the words in our sentence bear some relationship to each other, they are much easier to remember. Go ahead, try it. See how long it takes you to memorise the sentence as opposed to all the signs. This method is particularly easy when you remember some or all of the items but cannot remember their order.

*Remember*: make your sentence(s) memorable to you. Any sentence or series of words that helps you remember these letters will do. Here are just two more I created in a few seconds: A Tall Girl Called Lovely Vera Loved to Sip Sodas from Cans And Plates. Any Tiny Gerbil Could Love Venus; Long Silly Snakes Could All Pray. (Isn't it easy to make up memorably silly pictures in your head for these?)

You will find that in business or the classroom, mnemonic devices like this allow you readily to recall specific information that you need to retain for longer periods of time. They are used to remember chemical classifications, lines of music and anatomical lists.

As effective as mnemonic devices are, do not try to create them for everything you have to remember. Why? To generate a device for everything you need to learn would demand more time than any one person has. Also, you just might have trouble remembering all the devices you created to help you remember in the first place. Too many mnemonics can make your retention more complicated and hinder effective recall.

Complex mnemonics are not very useful – they can be too difficult to memorise. When you choose to create a mnemonic, you should keep it simple so that it facilitates the quick recall you intended.

Many people complain that their mind is a sieve – everything they read slips through; they never remember anything. I hope now you are convinced that this is a correctable problem. You do not have to be a genius to have good retention – you must be willing simply to work at gaining the skills that lead to proficient recall. As you master these skills, you will improve your reading by increasing your rate of retention.

# 10 *Build your own library*

If you are ever to become an active, avid reader, access to books
will do much to cultivate the habit. I suggest you 'build' your
own library. Your selections can and should reflect your own
tastes and interests, but try to make them wide and varied.
Include some of the classics, contemporary fiction, poetry and
biography.

Save your secondary school and college or university texts –
you will be amazed at how some of the material retains its
relevance. Also try to read a good newspaper every day so as
to keep up to date and informed.

Your local librarian can refer you to any number of lists of
the 'great books', most of which are available in inexpensive
paperback editions. Here are four more lists – compiled by
myself – of the 'great' classical authors; the 'great' not-so-
classical authors, poets and playwrights; some contemporary
'pretty good' writers and a selection of my own 'good' works.

You may want to incorporate these on your to buy list,
especially if you are planning a summer reading programme.

I am sure that I have left off someone's favourite author or
'important' title from these lists. So be it. They are not meant to
be comprehensive, just relatively representative. I doubt if anyone would disagree that a person familiar with the majority of
authors and works listed would be considered well read.

## Some 'great' classical authors

| | | | |
|---|---|---|---|
| Aeschylus | Cicero | S Johnson | Plato |
| Aesop | Confucius | Ben Jonson | Plutarch |
| Aquinas | Dante | Kant | Rousseau |
| Aristophanes | Descartes | Machiavelli | Shakespeare |
| Aristotle | Erasmus | Marx | Spinoza |
| Balzac | Flaubert | Milton | Virgil |
| Boccaccio | Goethe | Montaigne | Voltaire |
| J Caesar | Hegel | Nietzsche | |
| Cervantes | Homer | Ovid | |
| Chaucer | Horace | Pindar | |

## Some 'great' not-so-classical authors

| | |
|---|---|
| W H Auden | T S Eliot |
| Jane Austen | William Faulkner |
| Samuel Beckett | F Scott Fitzgerald |
| William Blake | E M Forster |
| Bertolt Brecht | Robert Frost |
| Charlotte Brontë | John Galsworthy |
| Emily Brontë | Jose Ortega y Gasset |
| Pearl Buck | Nikolai Gogol |
| Lord Byron | William Golding |
| Albert Camus | Maxim Gorky |
| Lewis Carroll | Thomas Hardy |
| Anton Chekov | Nathaniel Hawthorne |
| Joseph Conrad | Ernest Hemingway |
| e e cummings | Hermann Hesse |
| Daniel Defoe | Victor Hugo |
| Charles Dickens | Aldous Huxley |
| Emily Dickinson | Henrik Ibsen |
| Fyodor Dostoevsky | Washington Irving |
| Daphne du Maurier | Henry James |
| Arthur Conan Doyle | James Joyce |
| Theodore Dreiser | Franz Kafka |
| Alexandre Dumas | John Keats |
| George Eliot | Rudyard Kipling |

D H Lawrence

George Bernard Shaw

Harper Lee

Percy Bysshe Shelley

Laurie Lee

Richard Brinsley Sheridan

C S Lewis

Upton Sinclair

H W Longfellow

Alexander I Solzhenitsyn

James Russell Lowell

Edmund Spenser

Thomas Mann

Gertrude Stein

W Somerset Maugham

John Steinbeck

Herman Melville

Robert Louis Stevenson

H L Mencken

August Strindberg

Henry Miller

Jonathan Swift

A A Milne

Alfred Tennyson

John Milton

Dylan Thomas

H H Munro (Saki)

James Thurber

Vladimir Nabokov

J R R Tolkien

O Henry

Leo Tolstoy

Eugene O'Neill

Antony Trollope

George Orwell

Ivan Turgenev

Dorothy Parker

Mark Twain

Alan Paton

Robert Penn Warren

Boris Pasternak

Evelyn Waugh

Edgar Allan Poe

H G Wells

Ezra Pound

Walt Whitman

Marcel Proust

Oscar Wilde

Ellery Queen

Thornton Wilder

Erich Maria Remarque

Tennessee Williams

Bertrand Russell

P G Wodehouse

J D Salinger

Thomas Wolfe

George Sand

Virginia Woolf

Carl Sandburg

William Wordsworth

William Saroyan

William Butler Yeats

Jean-Paul Sartre

Emile Zola

## Some 'pretty good' contemporary authors

Edward Albee

John Barth

Kingsley Amis

Saul Bellow

Isaac Asimov

Anthony Burgess

J G Ballard

A S Byatt

Truman Capote
John Cheever
Roald Dahl
Don DeLillo
E L Doctorow
Frederick Forsyth
John Fowles
Günter Grass
Nadine Gordimer
Grahame Greene
Joseph Heller
Lillian Hellman
Barry Hines
Thomas Keneally
Milan Kundera
John LeCarré
Norman Mailer
Bernard Malamud

Gabriel Garcia Marquez
Arthur Miller
Toni Morrison
Joyce Carol Oates
Flannery O'Connor
John Osborne
Joe Orton
Thomas Pynchon
Philip Roth
Salman Rushdie
Isaac Bashevis Singer
Tom Stoppard
David Storey
William Styron
John Updike
Kurt Vonnegut
Alice Walker
Eudora Welty

## Some 'good' works

*The Adventures of Huckleberry Finn*
*The Adventures of Tom Sawyer*
*The Aeneid*
*Aesop's Fables*
*Alice in Wonderland*
*All Quiet on the Western Front*
*Animal Farm*
*Anna Karenina*
*A Room with a View*
*As I Lay Dying*
*Babbitt*
*Beloved*
*The Bonfire of the Vanities*
*Brave New World*
*Brighton Rock*
*The Brothers Karamazov*
*Bury My Heart at Wounded Knee*
*The Canterbury Tales*

*Catch-22*
*The Catcher in The Rye*
*Cider with Rosie*
*A Clockwork Orange*
*The Color Purple*
*Confessions of an English Opium Eater*
*The Count of Monte Cristo*
*Crime and Punishment*
*Cry, the Beloved Country*
*David Copperfield*
*Death In Venice*
*Death of a Salesman*
*The Diary of Anne Frank*
*Don Juan*
*Don Quixote*
*Dr Zhivago*
*Dr Jekyll and Mr Hyde*
*Ethan Fromme*

Far From the Madding Crowd
A Farewell to Arms
The Fixer
For Whom the Bell Tolls
The French Lieutenant's Woman
The Good Earth
The Grapes of Wrath
The Great Gatsby
Gulliver's Travels
Hamlet
Heart of Darkness
Hedda Gabler
The Hitchhiker's Guide to the
   Galaxy
The Hobbit
The Hounds of the Baskervilles
Howard's End
I, Claudius
The Illiad
The Invisible Man
Jane Eyre
Jude the Obscure
Julius Caesar
Kim
King Lear
Lady Chatterley's Lover
A Lesson Before Dying
The Lion, the Witch and the
   Wardrobe
A Long Day's Journey Into Night
Look Back in Anger
Lord Jim
The Lord of the Flies
The Lord of the Rings
Lucky Jim
Macbeth
Man and Superman
The Merchant of Venice
The Metamorphosis
Midnight's Children
Moby Dick
Mother Courage
Native Son

1984
Of Human Bondage
Of Mice and Men
The Old Man and the Sea
Oliver Twist
One Day in the Life of Ivan
   Denisovich
One Flew Over the Cuckoo's Nest
One Hundred Years of Solitude
Othello
Our Town
The Outsider
Paradise Lost
A Passage to India
The Pickwick Papers
The Picture of Dorian Gray
A Portrait of the Artist as a Young
   Man
Portrait of a Lady
Possession
Pride and Prejudice
The Prophet
The Ragged-trousered
   Philanthropist
Ragtime
'The Raven'
Rebecca
The Red Badge of Courage
The Remembrance of Things Past
The Return of the Native
'The Road Not Taken'
Robinson Crusoe
Romeo and Juliet
The Scarlet Letter
Siddhartha
Silas Marner
Sister Carrie
Slaughterhouse 5
Sons and Lovers
Sophie's Choice
The Sound and the Fury
Steppenwolf
A Streetcar Named Desire

The Sun Also Rises
The Tale of Genji
A Tale of Two Cities
Tender is the Night
Tess of the d'Urbervilles
The Thin Red Line
This Sporting Life
The Time Machine
The Tin Drum
To Kill a Mockingbird
Tom Jones
To the Lighthouse
Treasure Island

The Trial
2001 – A Space Odyssey
Ulysses
Vanity Fair
Walden
War and Peace
'The Wasteland'
Watership Down
Wind in the Willows
Winne-The-Pooh
Wuthering Heights
Zen and the Art of Motorcycle
   Maintenance

Reading every one of these books will undoubtedly make you a better reader; it will certainly make you more well read. The added bonus to establishing such a reading programme is an appreciation of certain authors, books, cultural events and the like that separates the cultured from the merely educated and the undereducated.

Read on and enjoy.

# 11 Reading: a lifelong activity

Well, you made it to the end of the book. I hope you found the motivation – whether intrinsic or extrinsic – to define your purpose, discern the important details, grasp the main idea and retain what you read. I promised not to preach about the joys of reading. And I haven't... too much.

Your need to read – and comprehend and retain what you read – will not end when you leave school, college or university.

Planning on working? From the very first week, when you are handed the company policy guide, you will be expected to seek out the facts and read critically – and know what statements such as, 'Our dress code requires professional attire at all times', mean.

Business proposals, annual reports, patient charts, corporate profiles, product reports, sales reports, budget proposals, business plans, CVs, complaints letters, inter-office memos – no matter what type of work you do, you will not be able to avoid the avalanche of paper and required reading that accompanies it.

Not only will your job require the ability to read and comprehend, but so will other facets of your life. If you plan to own your home, wait until you see the pile of paperwork you will have to wade through.

Credit card applications? Better read the fine print to make sure you know when your payments must be in... Insurance policies, appliance warranties, local ordinances, newspapers, membership applications and tax forms – it appears that any goal you pursue in your life will need you to scale mountains of reading material.

For your own best interest, you must be prepared to read – and understand.

I wish you the greatest possible success in your future reading pursuits, of which there will be many... throughout your life.

# Index